Xmas 2007
To my precious friend,
We must do lunch
again soon!
Love Margy

A Year at Les Fougères

Charles Part & Jennifer Warren-Part

Design and layout: Katrina Moy
Photographs (unless otherwise noted): Andrew Van Beek (photoVanBeek)
www.photovanbeek.com
Staff photographs (unless otherwise noted): Charles Part, Jennifer Warren-Part
and staff.

Published by Chelsea Books
Chelsea, Quebec
www.chelseabooks.ca

Library and Archives Canada Cataloguing in Publication

Part, Charles, 1956-
A year at les Fougères / Charles Part and Jennifer Warren-Part.

ISBN 978-0-9781602-6-5

1. Cookery. 2. Fougères (Restaurant) I. Warren-Part, Jennifer, 1957-
II. Title.

TX714.P3765 2007 641.5   C2007-905587-7

For Alec and Beverly
and with thanks to all members of
the Les Fougères family,
past, present and future.

Acknowledgements

Katrina Moy has been a tireless, creative and skilled partner in the overall production of this book, while at the same time somehow meeting the many demands of her job as manager of Les Fougères. Thank you.

For over a year, photographer Andrew Van Beek came to chronicle what was happening at Les Fougères and to visually record recipes at different stages. Almost all the photographs in this book are his. He was enormously patient and professional and has beautifully captured our passage through a year. Thank you.

Our main readers were Jake and Joan Warren and we thank them for so thoroughly and incisively going through the text and their sensitive and invaluable suggestions. Frances Curry, Susie Leamen and Chris Marriott proofread the manuscript and we thank them for their efforts and contributions. Thank you to Stephanie Moy-Shuster for her layout advice.

As a passionate young wannabe chef back in the seventies, I always had the dream of running a country restaurant. I realized that this was an ambition that would take lots of hard work, experience, patience, time, money and someone to share and enjoy the same dream by working with me to achieve it.

In 1981, after several years of running a restaurant in the family store in London, England, I moved to Canada and met Jennifer (the sister of an old school chum). It was obvious that she had the same kind of passion, even if she was still working for the Ontario Government as a trade policy advisor.

In 1986, we opened a small neighborhood restaurant in the Beaches area of Toronto and, despite the backdrop of an economy in recession, we enjoyed this demanding venture with all its new challenges.

Our two children arrived and we felt the call to leave the city in order to raise Alec and Beverly in an environment closer to nature. Toronto was getting more congested, crime was up and the endless streetcars rattling past the front door seemed to add to the stress of running a restaurant in a city.

Jennifer had grown up very close to Ottawa in the beautiful Gatineau Hills. This seemed an ideal choice if we could pull it off. Here was a region that was only twelve minutes from downtown Ottawa/Gatineau, five minutes to the ski hills at Camp Fortune and next to wonderful bike paths, hiking, cross country ski trails and beautiful lakes and rivers for canoeing, kayaking and fishing.

We found our dream location on a lovely two-acre wooded lot in Chelsea, Québec and it has now been 15 years since the conception of Restaurant Les Fougères. Time flies when you're having fun – this book describes some of the recipes and seasonal changes we have enjoyed along the way.

Charles Part
July 2007

When we moved to Chelsea, Québec with our young children from Toronto 15 years ago, we knew we were buying a country gas station and that we were going to renovate it into a restaurant. We were not sure how it would work out but knew that, whatever happened, we four were together, had a lot of support from family, were passionate about a career in fine food and that we would cope. In any case, we wanted out of the city and so were well ahead of the game no matter what.

What happened was better than we could have ever hoped. Our children have grown up in a most beautiful corner of the world under the watchful eye of a generous and caring community; kindred spirits, now friends, have joined us in building Les Fougères – in the restaurant, the store, the gardens, the cellar and the all important (though generally invisible) office. As well, people from our community and region, and visitors from away, have supported us with their visits over many years.

Right from the beginning, the power of our surroundings and of the seasons were shaping our sensibilities and possibilities and were becoming something very integral to ourselves and our work. Before long we found ourselves rooted in this beautiful place. Happily anchored, as we had never been before, we could take ourselves and our project more seriously than simply as something that might or might not work. We set out to try to create a special place of natural peace, beauty, hospitality and nourishment for body and soul.

Some time ago we decided to collect recipes and observations about what happened at Les Fougères over the course of a year in an effort to capture the way the land and seasons shape our lives and work.

Our sense of awe and thanks at having found ourselves with our feet on the ground at Les Fougères is what made us want to write this book.

Jennifer Warren-Part
July 2007

Table of Contents

January

Deflating balloons suspended in mid-air after December 31st's celebrations is the nostalgic sight which greets us as we arrive at the restaurant on the first day of January. New Year's Eve was quite a party and we still feel caught up in the middle ground between looking forward and looking back.

As things begin to get squared away again, we settle into a rhythm different from that of the high days and holidays of December. The restaurant is less busy and will remain so for a few months as many people seem to hibernate. The pace slows a bit and there is time to dream, to think, and then to plan.

This is such a beautiful time at the restaurant – the sight of long shadows falling across the snow through the naked woods, of black-capped chickadees and nuthatches darting back and forth between feeders and nearby bushes, of a blazing fire in our granite fireplace and of the sense of peace and warmth shared while enjoying cassoulet by candlelight as the snow falls silently outside.

Something we always associate with January and which begins to call us back to action is the fleeting availability of bitter Seville oranges. For a few weeks in January we are all thrown into a frenzy of marmalade making. We make about 800 jars every year in our store kitchen and the gorgeous, sharp, astringent smell of Seville orange is emblematic of

the January air at Les Fougères as the marmalade gently simmers day and night. Our marmalade is made in the traditional way without added pectin. There is something beautiful and parable-like in the symmetry of marmalade making – every orange has just enough natural pectin in its seeds and skin to set its own juice and chopped peel to a perfect gel. Nothing is added except sugar (and, of course, a splash of Scotch whiskey at the end). Everything is held in perfect natural balance.

The slower pace allows us to hold cooking classes in the Store. We will also put the final touches on our new Winter Menu. Winter may not be much of a growing season in this northern country but now is the time to reap the harvest of the condiments and preserves we put up in summer and fall, and to enjoy using root vegetables and some of the bounty of harvests occurring elsewhere – besides Seville oranges we can savour blood oranges and other citrus now in peak condition. We enjoy dipping into fresh spices from far away and think ourselves extremely lucky to be able to celebrate what is vibrant and local but also to seek out the best from wherever it hails, the range and availability of which is expressive of our multicultural Canadianness itself.

The new winter menu will involve comforting soups, deeply satisfying braises and casseroles, curry and cassoulet, caramelized root vegetables, big wines, hot desserts, dried fruits and cheeses as well as our homemade condiments and preserves. Rather than despairing of the lack of fresh local produce, we see and delight in a different range of possibilities and techniques. Indeed, we love the distinct seasons we have. We cook, eat, drink, dress, play and move around differently in every season and we are all the richer and happier for this.

The first real cold snap arrives as the thermometer plummets to minus thirty and beyond. Even the birds don't come to the feeders – they stay inside the fir trees with their feathers fluffed up for warmth. Save for the squeak of our step on the dry-packed snow there is not a sound. Then the stillness is broken with a signature northern sound – the earsplitting sound of a tree cracking in the deep freeze as ice crystals form, expand and explode within the wood. This causes the bark to snap and shrink with a sound like rifle shot shattering the quiet in the frozen dead of night.

Then the astonishing absence of sound returns. The air is never as clear as on these bright days when it is even too frigid to snow. The nights are as breathtaking for the cold as they are for the clarity of numberless stars in the sky bowl above us.

In our region, the Gatineau Park land is a maze of wild and beautiful groomed cross-country skiing trails dotted with rustic ski-in cabins. Sometimes prepared foods from our store find their way into backpacks and we love the picture we have in our mind's eye of Les Fougères soups, casseroles, curries and tourtières being warmed in cabin woodstoves all across the Hills.

Hare Ragoût
with Seville Orange and Rosemary Gnocchi

6 servings

We source our hare from trappers in La Petite-Nation region east of Chelsea. The meat is darker and more flavourful than rabbit. The Seville and rosemary accents in the tender gnocchi bring welcome orange and herbal notes to the rich ragoût. These gnocchi are also wonderful simply tossed in butter with sautéed pancetta and shavings of a nice nutty cheese like Parmigiano Reggiano or Gré des Champs, the artisanal raw milk cheese from Saint-Jean-sur-Richelieu, south of Montréal.

Hare ragoût

1 hare, jointed
½ cup olive oil
2 tbsp butter
6 ounces lardon bacon
1 large cooking onion, diced
1 large carrot, diced
6 whole garlic cloves, peeled
2 tbsp tomato paste
4 chopped tomatoes
2 tbsp of red currant jelly
¼ cup balsamic vinegar
½ bottle of white wine
2 tbsp crushed juniper
   berries
leaves from 2 sprigs of
   fresh thyme
3 bay leaves
salt and freshly ground
   black pepper

In a heavy bottomed, oven-proof casserole, heat olive oil, butter and bacon over medium-high heat until fat has been rendered from the bacon.

Add the hare pieces to the casserole and brown well on all sides. Season with salt and pepper. Add onion, carrot and garlic cloves and continue to cook, stirring occasionally, until vegetables have started to brown. Add tomato paste, tomatoes, redcurrant jelly, balsamic vinegar, white wine, juniper berries, thyme and bay leaves.

Cover with lid and cook in the oven at 375°F for 1 hour or until hare is tender.

Seville orange and rosemary gnocchi

3 Yukon Gold potatoes
2 eggs
1 egg yolk
1 tbsp olive oil
1 tbsp fresh chopped
  rosemary
2 tbsp Seville orange
  marmalade
lemon zest
orange zest
1 cup flour
butter
1 cup grated Gré des
  Champs or
  Parmigiano Reggiano
  (to serve)

Bake the potatoes in their skins. Let rest until cool enough to handle, then spoon out flesh and pass it through a ricer.

Mound the riced potato onto a floured board. Make a well in the centre and add the eggs, egg yolk, olive oil, rosemary, marmalade and zests. Using a fork stir all the ingredients in the well together, incorporating the potato bit by bit. Gradually add just enough flour to form a tender dough and knead gently and briefly to form a ball.

Divide dough into quarters. Roll each quarter into a $\frac{1}{4}$" rope and cut into pieces on the diagonal. Throw into boiling salted water. As soon as gnocchi rise to the top, strain and toss with butter.

To serve:

Spoon into serving bowls and serve with a ladle of hare ragout, grated Gré des Champs or Parmigiano Reggiano and a garnish of fresh rosemary and orange zest.

Seville Orange Marmalade

Makes approx eight 16-ounce jars

Life without buttered brown toast and sharp Seville orange marmalade – maybe with a few rashers of bacon on top – just would not quite reach its potential… We have many real marmalade addicts who visit the store regularly to stock up. Bitter Seville oranges from Spain are only available for a few weeks at the beginning of the year.

10 Seville oranges
$1\frac{1}{2}$ pounds sugar
$\frac{1}{4}$ cup Scotch whiskey
   (optional)

Place oranges in large pot and cover with cold water. Bring to boil and simmer gently for 2 hours. Remove from heat and let rest until cool enough to handle.

Remove oranges from water with a slotted spoon. Reserve the cooking water. Slice each orange in half and scrape out the flesh and the pips. Discard the bitter white membrane. Cover the pips and flesh with boiling water and let sit at room temperature overnight. Process the orange peel to a fine chop in a food processor and return it to the cooking water. Refrigerate and reserve.

Next day, place chopped peel and cooking water in a large heavy pot. Press the pip mixture through a sieve over the pot so that all the gel extracted from the pips overnight is added to the chopped orange peel mixture. Discard the pips. Add the sugar and boil briskly, skimming away froth, until marmalade has thickened. To test, place a spoonful of marmalade on a small plate and refrigerate for 5 minutes. Test consistency and continue cooking if gel has not been reached.

When the marmalade has reached the desired thickness, stir in Scotch Whiskey.

Pour into hot sterilized jars and seal.

Rack of Lamb with Seville and Seaweed Jus

6 servings

The unique bitter-sweet flavour of Seville orange marmalade is used here to give rich lamb jus a beguiling lift. This recipe derives from an old Welsh recipe which uses coastal seaweed with Seville orange to sauce lamb – the seaweed bringing its unique accent to the dish but also underscoring the sea-saltiness of the Welsh coast-raised lamb. The delicious pre-salé lamb from Québec's Isle-Verte would be a perfect choice if you can find it. These lambs graze on the salt marsh margins of the island where high water and sea air bathes their pasture with salt, giving the meat wonderful flavour and moistness. If you can't get L'Isle-Verte lamb, use fresh local lamb and enjoy the seashore lacing and deep orange notes of the seaweed and the marmalade.

4 racks of lamb

3 lbs of lamb bones/trim

2 whole onions, quartered

1 whole head of garlic, cut in half horizontally

1½ cups white wine

6-ounce sheet of dried kelp (Asian grocery)

4 tbsp Seville orange marmalade

3 ounces cold butter, cut into cubes

salt and freshly ground black pepper

To make lamb stock, place lamb bones in a roasting pan with the onions and the garlic. Roast in the oven at 400°F for one hour. Transfer the bones to a large pot. Deglaze the roasting pan with the wine, scraping all the browned bits from the bottom of the pan and adding this to the saucepan with the bones. Cover bones and vegetables with cold water. Add kelp. Bring to a boil over high heat, reduce heat to low and skim off any foam and fat that has accumulated. Simmer lamb stock for 1½ hours, then strain through a cheesecloth. Discard solids.

Place racks of lamb in a clean roasting pan. Roast in the oven at 375°F for about 20 minutes for medium-rare. Remove lamb from roasting pan to a plate, cover with foil and let rest.

Meanwhile, deglaze the roasting pan with 3 cups of the lamb stock. Simmer over medium heat to reduce by half. Add the marmalade and butter and keep reducing to a glaze. Adjust salt and pepper to taste.

To serve, cut the racks into chops and nap with sauce.

Pink Grapefruit Soufflé

6 servings

Like Seville oranges, pink grapefruit are often at their peak in January. This is perhaps one of our most favourite desserts EVER! The fruit flavour is strong, pure and tangy. The exterior of the soufflé has a slight crunch and the interior is molten. The mouthwatering pure grapefruit flavour and the contrasts in texture and temperature will bring you to your knees... This recipe comes courtesy of former pastry chef and critically acclaimed artisanal baker Kevin Mathieson (www.art-is-in-bakery.com).

1 cup fresh pink grapefruit juice
$\frac{1}{4}$ cup whipping cream
2 egg yolks
2 tbsp sugar, divided
1 tbsp cornstarch
1 tsp pink grapefruit zest
8 egg whites

Grease six 6-ounce ramekins right to the top with melted butter. Coat the insides lightly and evenly with sugar.

Preheat oven to 400°F.

Grapefruit custard:

Bring grapefruit juice to a boil over medium heat, reduce heat to low and continue to simmer until reduced by half. Keep the heat low because the juice discolours easily. Whisk in cream, yolks, 1 tbsp sugar, cornstarch and zest. Increase heat to medium and return to a boil, stirring constantly. Boil for 1 minute then remove from heat and cool completely to room temperature. Keep covered with plastic wrap to prevent skin forming.

To assemble soufflés:

Whip egg whites with remaining 1 tbsp sugar until they hold firm peaks. Stir the grapefruit custard with a rubber spatula to smooth, and gradually fold in the beaten whites slowly and delicately until completely combined. Fill the ramekins to two-thirds full with the soufflé mixture.

Bake for 15-20 minutes until soufflés are puffed and golden. Dust sifted icing sugar on top and serve immediately. The soufflés should have a lovely molten interior.

Next page: Making Seville orange and rosemary
gnocchi with hare ragoût

January is the time for making Seville orange marmalade. Each batch is made by hand with the addition of only sugar - and Scotch whiskey, of course.

Rack of lamb with a Seville orange and seaweed jus

Cooking classes in the store

Pink grapefruit soufflé

February

As February begins we are still in a deep freeze. Besides woodpecker tapping, isolated nocturnal owl hoots, or the occasional bird call – certainly no birdsong at this time of year – the outside sounds come mostly from the wind causing branches and brittle, tenacious oak and beech leaves to rub and rattle against each other.

This is a time of stripped down and deeply affecting beauty. There are no heart-bending frills, Easter-egg colours or head-turning fragrances. This is the stark beauty of wind-bare trees, of animal movements and bird lift-offs perfectly imprinted in virgin snow, and of the clock face movement of deep blue shadows angled across the snow as the cold sun passes overhead. Sunlight and moonlight also surprise us with unexpected mauve and blue colours when their refracting and absorbing canvas is snow and ice.

On a particularly cold morning on the way to the restaurant we notice a huge shimmering ring around the sun with bright mirror orbs at each side. This extraordinary phenomenon, sometimes called a "prairie sun" signals a remarkably clear and frigid day ahead. On another morning we are surprised by a raven-sized pileated woodpecker darting out of the woods in front of the car, seemingly leading us down the road to the restaurant before cutting sharply back into the woods. The striking scarlet crest of this large, year-round woodland resident needs to be seen to be believed.

Depending on weather and availability of food elsewhere we may be lucky enough to welcome waves of occasional migrants to our bird feeders such as red polls, goldfinches and pine siskins. Regular feeders continue to be chickadees, nuthatches, woodpeckers and blue jays…not to mention the squirrels.

Valentine's Day livens up the month and we present a lovely romantic menu – rarely avoiding the temptations of love apples and passion fruit. Ironically, although it is the occasion for which we receive the most requests for reservations, it cannot be an overly crowded night because almost all of the reservations are, of course, for couples, even if the table normally seats four or six. It is also not a noisy night of revelry but a singularly quiet time of sweet whisperings. There is often a proposal and we feel privileged to be part of this magical time.

In our region at this time of year the Winterlude festival celebrates mid-winter in all its unique beauty with activities such as skating, ice sculpture, dog sledding, ice fishing, ice slides and fireworks. Winterlude, as well as cross-country skiing events such as the Keskinada Loppet, bring visitors pouring into our region to participate, compete and enjoy. Some of these welcome visitors come in to unwind by our fire and partake of heartwarming food and wines.

By the end of February we are definitely noticing that the mornings are brightening and the days are a little longer. We are spending time with our seed catalogues and deciding what to plant at Les Fougères and what to ask our partner farmers to plant for us this coming spring. Les Fougères is a two-acre property and we have beds for vegetables, greens, herbs and edible flowers. We are not large enough to supply all the restaurant's needs, which come mainly from local farms during the growing season, but we do try to focus ourselves on specialized produce and garnishes we find hard to source elsewhere. These items, such as heirloom tomatoes, patty pan squashes, specialty beets, chards, kale and radishes, sweet cicely, salad burnett, lemon verbena, chervil, sweet woodruff and so on, will become important accents in our summer dishes. We will place our seed orders now and soon will begin sowing indoors or in Jenny's nearby greenhouse so we will have strong seedlings ready for spring planting – this is the start of real "slow food".

Brandade de Morue

6 servings

Brandade de morue is a purée of salt cod with potatoes, olive oil, garlic, lemon and wine. It is sublime. Historically, cod (much of it from our east coast) was salted and provided a cheap and lasting source of protein along maritime trade and conquest routes – ironically making cod, a northern fish, very important in Mediterranean and Caribbean cuisines. The stories of cod, spices, salt and conquest are all intertwined.

1 pound deboned salt cod fillets

1 onion, chopped

6 cloves peeled garlic

2 stalks celery, chopped

1 large potato, peeled and chopped

6 black peppercorns

4 bay leaves

1 lemon, cut in quarters with seeds removed

2 cups white wine

1 cup water

juice of 1 lemon

1 clove garlic

1 cup extra-virgin olive oil

Cover the salt cod with water and soak for 24 hours. Drain and rinse the fillets well.

Place all the remaining ingredients except the lemon juice, a single clove of garlic and the oil in a heavy bottomed pot with a lid and steam gently until the potatoes are cooked and soft.

Place drained cod fillets on potato mixture, replace lid and continue to steam until cod is cooked and fork-tender – about 10 minutes.

Remove bay leaves and pieces of lemon from cod mixture. Place mixture in processor and pulse with reserved garlic and lemon juice until texture is smooth. Meanwhile, reduce any remaining cooking liquid to a syrup over medium heat. Transfer brandade to a bowl and slowly whisk in olive oil and reduced syrup.

Serve with baguette as an appetizer or use as starch for a fish dish.

Brandade Soup with White Truffle Oil

8 servings

For this recipe we are steaming the building blocks of brandade together with good stock, celery, bay leaf, peppercorns and a touch of cream to produce a soup with subtle and haunting flavours of cod and sea salt coming through wine-steamed garlic and vegetables. Although the roots of brandade link it to Canadian waters, brandade is often part of a traditional Christmas Eve spread in the south of France where it may be festively garnished with sliced truffles. We drizzle white truffle oil on our soup following this felicitous idea.

1 pound deboned salt cod fillets

½ pound peeled chopped potatoes

2 lemons, chopped and seeded

2 bay leaves

¾ cup peeled garlic cloves

½ tbsp black peppercorns

1 celery heart, chopped

4 cups chicken stock

2 cups white wine

2 cups water

salt and freshly ground black pepper to taste

½ cup whipping cream, if desired

white truffle oil for garnish

Soak cod in cold water overnight. Drain and rinse well.

Place cod in heavy-bottomed pot with potatoes, lemons, bay leaves, garlic, peppercorns and celery. Cover with chicken stock, white wine and water. Bring to a boil, then reduce heat to medium and simmer gently until ingredients are soft.

Remove bay leaves. Purée in food processor with cream until smooth. Check consistency and add more stock and cream, if necessary. Season to taste with salt and pepper. Bring back to boil and serve drizzled with white truffle oil.

Valentine's Menu

Kir Royal au cassis, aux fraises ou aux pêches

❧

Leek & Stilton soup, garnished with toasted hazelnuts
Gewurztraminer Réserve 2002 Alsace, Dopff & Irion

❧

Haricots vert salad with homemade Arctic char gravlax
Sauvignon Blanc 2002 Marlborough, Babich

❧

P.E.I. scallops, Black Tiger shrimp and mussels served en nage
with saffron and basil, with brunoise of fennel, potatoes and tomatoes
Tokay Pinot Gris 2002 Alsace, Vignerons de Pfaffenheim
or
Escalope of venison with cassis jus, served with potato & chèvre purée,
fresh thyme, and grilled courgette
Cabernet Sauvignon 2001 Niagara Peninsula, Pillitteri
or
Confit of Quebec duck served on roesti potato with
Papineauville goat's cheese, poached pear and spinach
Madiran Torus 2001, Alain Brumont

❧

Passionfruit crème brûlée with chocolate truffle and biscuits
Riesling Indian Summer 2001 Niagara Peninsula, Cave Spring Cellars

Coffee or tea

Cassoulet

6 servings

The Languedoc region in France is the origin of this comforting and delicious dish, so perfect for a cold night. White beans are simmered for hours with goose, cured and preserved sausage, pork hock, herbs, mustard, maple syrup and wine. Beans are a perfect conduit for all the flavours and aromatics where they intermingle and amplify during the long simmering. The types of white beans listed in the recipe are best because the beans do not break down in the long cooking. We serve the cassoulet in a bowl topped with crisped duck leg confit.

4 cups dry white beans
(such as Great
Northern, Lingots or
Tarbais)

1 goose, cut into pieces

2 large onions, chopped

2 sticks celery, chopped

12 whole garlic cloves,
peeled

1 whole smoked pork
hock, split

8 ounces belly bacon,
cut into lardons

1 cup ale

1½ cups dry white wine

½ cup Dijon mustard

2 tbsp duck fat

6 bay leaves

1 tbsp whole black
peppercorns

1 tbsp fresh thyme

stock or water to cover

Soak beans in water overnight. Rinse and drain. Place the beans in a large oven-proof pot with a tight-fitting lid.

Place the goose pieces on the beans. Surround the goose with onions, celery, garlic, pork hock and lardons. Mix the ale, mustard and white wine together and pour over top. Add the duck fat, bay leaves, peppercorns and thyme. Cover with stock or water and place the lid on the pot.

Bring to a simmer over medium heat, then move into a 375°F oven for 2½ to 3 hours to simmer gently until beans are tender. Halfway through, add sausages, confit, maple syrup and balsamic vinegar. Add more liquid (wine, stock and/or water) at this point if the mixture appears to be getting dry.

6 assorted smoked & cured
   pork & garlic sausages, i.e
   Toulouse, Kielbasa each
   cut in 4
½ cup maple syrup
4 tbsp balsamic vinegar
6 legs duck confit
   (recipe follows)

To serve:

To serve, ladle into large shallow bowls, top each serving with a leg of duck confit
(recipe follows).

Confit of Québec Moulard Duck

with Roesti Potato, Sautéed Spinach, Poached Pear and Papineauville Goat's Cheese from Ferme Floralpe

6 servings

Still our most popular dish, and has been ever since we first started serving it at our former restaurant, "Loons" in the Beaches area of Toronto – so for over 20 years now. The sweetness and tenderness of the "confit-ed" duck leg and the soft pear is counterpointed by the tang of Papineauville goat's cheese and spinach and the crunchiness of the roesti potato and crisped duck skin – a delicious partnership of opposites in flavour and texture.

We use the leg of the Moulard duck which is raised specifically for its foie gras. To "confit" means to cook gently in its own fat and then preserve in this fat. Contrary to what many think, this does not produce a fatty or greasy dish. The confit method actually allows the duck to render away its thick layer of fat leaving a beautifully crispy skin and a meat which is fork-tender and succulent. That you can make duck confit and leave it sealed in fat in your fridge for months makes it the most convenient gourmet fast food – ready to be heated up and served as above or on top of a salad…on a pizza crust…in pasta and in so many other ways at a moment's notice. In short, you are mad not to have a few containers of duck confit in the back of your fridge at all times!

Duck Confit

6 duck legs (preferably
   Moulard)
coarse salt
melted duck fat or lard
   to cover
¾ cup goat's cheese
aged balsamic vinegar
fresh thyme
orange zest

Rub duck legs with coarse salt and leave in fridge overnight. Wipe excess salt off legs.

Place in heavy-bottomed pan and cover with melted duck fat or lard. Simmer very gently for 2-3 hours or until the flesh draws back towards the joint leaving the bone clean for about 1 inch.

Gently remove duck from fat and place in crock. Pour fat over to completely cover and seal duck. Chill and refrigerate.

To serve, remove duck carefully from fat. Place leg skin side up in pan and place in oven at 400°F for 7 minutes. Turn duck over (skin side down) for another 7 minutes until the skin is golden brown and crispy.

Roesti potato

2 potatoes
6 tbsp duck fat
salt and pepper

Grate peeled potatoes. Heat fat in sauté pan. Place a pile of grated potato into pan and season with salt and pepper. When golden, flip to other side. When both sides are golden, remove from pan.

Sautéed spinach

2 bags spinach
$\frac{1}{4}$ cup water
2 tbsp melted butter
salt and pepper

Remove stems from spinach and rinse well in cold water to remove any grit. Place spinach in a pot with water and let it wilt over medium heat. Remove cooked spinach from pot and drain. Brush melted butter over spinach and season to taste.

Poached pears

3 pears
$\frac{1}{2}$ cup sugar
cold water to cover
juice of $\frac{1}{2}$ lemon
2 tbsp butter

Peel pears. Place pears, sugar, water and lemon in pot and bring to a boil over high heat. Reduce heat to medium-low and simmer until pears are tender. Leave to cool. Slice pears in half and remove core and stem. Slice each half into 3 pieces lengthwise. Heat butter in sauté pan. Add pear pieces and sauté until golden.

To serve:

Place roesti in centre of warm plate surrounded by a ring of spinach and 3-4 sautéed pear slices. Place 2 tbsp of fresh goat's cheese in centre of roesti and top with a confit-ed duck leg. Sprinkle confit with a little aged balsamic vinegar, fresh thyme and orange zest.

Crème Brûlée

8 servings

A classic – gently cooked over a bain-marie (not baked!) – this sublime, just-set volup-tuous custard is made, of course, with the inimitable flavour and telltale black specks of real vanilla bean. The thin wafer of brittle caramel on top makes the custard seem even creamier by contrast. We also use this custard as the base for all our homemade ice creams at the restaurant and store.

4 cups whipping cream
$\frac{1}{4}$ vanilla bean
12 egg yolks
$\frac{1}{3}$ cup sugar

Place cream in large stainless steel mixing bowl. Slice vanilla bean lengthwise and scrape out seeds into cream. Place pod in cream as well, and scald cream in the bowl over a pan of simmering water.

Whisk egg yolks and sugar in another bowl. Add a little of the scalded cream, whisking until combined and warm. Pour egg yolk mixture back into the bowl of scalded cream and whisk to combine.

Cook this mixture over the simmering water, stirring frequently, until thickened to the point where it coats the back of a spoon. Remove from heat and pour into eight 6-ounce ramekins. Place in fridge to cool and set, ideally overnight.

To serve:

Sprinkle top with sugar and caramelize with a blow torch. Alternatively, moisten 1 cup sugar in a pan with a little water. Bring to boil and simmer until sugar has become a light amber caramel. Pour a thin layer of this caramel on top of each cooled and set custard.

To garnish as in photo:

Serve with caramel twists (page 90), tuile cigarettes (page 62) and a cassis jelly (page 69). To make white chocolate hearts, gently melt white chocolate and place in a squeeze bottle. Squeeze heart shapes onto a parchment-lined baking tray. Chill to set in fridge, then <u>carefully</u> peel away from paper.

Top: Steaming salt cod for brandade
Bottom: Drizzling brandade soup with white truffle oil

Ingredients for cassoulet include goose, ham hock, local maple syrup, Québec microbrewery ale, Ontario wine and locally made sausages

Crisped duck confit on long-simmered cassoulet garnished with fresh thyme and orange zest

Québec duck confit served on roesti potato with
Ferme Floralpe goat's cheese, sautéed spinach and pears

Following page: Woodland shadows across the snow;
crème brûlée with biscuits and a cassis jelly

March

Sometime in the early days of March the icicles around the restaurant begin to shine with melting water in the late afternoon sun – yes, the icicles are melting, and yes, there is the welcome surprise of slanting sunlight late into the afternoon.

The days at last are getting longer and spirits lift. In a few weeks we will reach spring equinox – night will equal day and then yield to longer sunlit hours. What was dormant begins slowly to come alive again.

The air has softened and there is even a little warmth in the sun. Indeed, our last cross-country skiing forays of the season are now likely to have keeping cool as more of a preoccupation than keeping warm. Other signs of winter's retreat are everywhere: grosbeaks, finches, pine siskins, red polls and other migrants are stocking up at the birdfeeders; saucers of thaw are beginning to appear in the snow around the base of trees as sapwood comes alive; the seeds we've ordered to start many of our vegetables and flowers for summer have arrived and are planted out in seedling flats. With warmer days and yet still freezing nights, sap begins to rise and the tapping of sugar maple trees has begun: fires are stoked in sugar shacks throughout the region as clear sap is boiled down by forty times its original volume to produce one of Nature's purest northern gifts – maple syrup.

At Les Fougères, March is a special month of renewal. We open the restaurant only on weekends so we can clean, scrub, take apart, strip, repaint and refresh the restaurant during the early part of the week but also leave time for everyone to have a break before a busy spring and summer ahead. The whole Fougères team rolls up its sleeves during this period and our spring clean is a strenuous but satisfying group effort which keeps the place spotless and humming and all of us strongly connected with our physical space and with each other.

For us, March is the month that straddles winter and spring. It brings our last chance to cook up some of the heartier warming dishes of the colder weather months but also looks forward to such harbingers of spring as the shocking pink of the first forced Québec rhubarb, fresh local maple syrup and the greater availability of sablefish and northern halibut in Canadian waters.

By the end of the month our annual cleaning and break are behind us and our seedlings are beginning to sprout. Outside, the apple trees have been pruned and some branches have been brought to inside vases where they will burgeon with tender leaves. Forced daffodils also fill the windowsills at Les Fougères with the promise of coming spring.

On March 31st a first surprising thunder and lightening storm sweeps across the region, taking with it much of the remaining snow. We look out over the still frozen but now thaw-blistered Gatineau River and across to the Hills. We begin to make out the slightest loom in the treetops as the collectivity of tiny shoots and buds begin to swell. We see our first robin, mourning doves and redwing blackbirds; we hear the first few Canada geese overhead, scouting out the readiness of the northern migratory route. Encouraged by all around us we feel energized and full of anticipation. This feels like the real beginning of the New Year to us.

Pan-Seared Québec Moulard Duck Foie Gras
with Rhubarb and Rosemary Compote

4 servings

Québec is the only region in Canada that raises Moulard ducks for foie gras. We love pairing the richness of seared duck foie gras with the tartness of rhubarb – so perfect at this time of year when the first forced rhubarb is beginning to be available. The savoury piney-ness of rosemary is a lovely herbal accent.

4 slices of chilled fresh foie
   gras, 2 ounces each
flour seasoned with a
   little salt and pepper
fresh chopped rosemary
fleur de sel

Dust foie gras slices lightly with seasoned flour. Sear foie gras on a hot grill pan or sauté pan for 30 seconds per side or until exterior is nicely coloured and interior feels molten and warm.

Rhubarb rosemary compote

4 stalks fresh rhubarb
   chopped into 1" pieces
$\frac{1}{2}$ cup water
zest of $\frac{1}{2}$ orange
$\frac{1}{2}$ cup red currant jelly
$\frac{1}{4}$ cup balsamic vinegar
$\frac{1}{4}$ cup sugar
$\frac{1}{2}$ tsp freshly cracked
   black pepper
1 tsp chopped fresh
   rosemary

Place chopped rhubarb and water in a heavy bottomed pot over medium-high heat. Bring to a simmer, reduce heat to medium and cook gently until rhubarb has softened. Add remaining ingredients and simmer until rhubarb is tender and jelly has melted. Adjust seasoning and/or add a little sugar to taste if necessary.

To serve:

Season foie gras with a little chopped fresh rosemary and fleur de sel. Serve with rhubarb rosemary compote. A small roesti potato would also be a nice accompaniment (page 31).

Panfried Wild Arctic Char with a Maple and Balsamic Glaze

served on Parsnip Purée with a Pink Grapefruit and Ginger Jus

6 servings

Arctic char is a relative of the salmon but does not migrate out to sea for several years as the wild Atlantic salmon does. It is the most northerly-occurring fish, spending its time in the lakes, rivers and estuaries of the north. We generally source our wild char from Baffin Island through Pangnirtung. It has a deep pink colour, moist flake and sweet flavour. The pairing with parsnip and pink grapefruit and a glaze of maple-balsamic offers a delicious tart-sweet backdrop for the fish.

Parsnip purée

6 parsnips, peeled and
   chopped
½ cup butter
½ cup whipping cream
¼ cup sherry
zest of half an orange
grated nutmeg, salt and
   pepper to taste

Cover parsnips with cold water in a large pot and bring to a boil over high heat. Reduce heat to low and simmer, uncovered, until tender. Drain. Purée in food processor until very smooth. Add remaining ingredients and process again until just combined.

Maple-balsamic glaze

1 cup maple syrup
1 cup balsamic vinegar

Place syrup and vinegar in a heavy-bottomed pot. Bring to a boil over high heat, then reduce heat to low and simmer until reduced to a syrupy consistency.

Grapefruit ginger jus

1 cup fresh pink grapefruit
   juice
1½ cups chicken stock
¾ cup white wine
2 tbsp sliced sweet pickled
   ginger (see page 110)
¼ cup thinly sliced leek
   rings
¼ cup thinly sliced red
   onion
½ cup cold butter, cubed

Place juice, stock, wine and ginger in a heavy-bottomed pot and bring to a boil over high heat. Reduce heat to low and simmer until reduced by half. Add leek rings and red onion and continue to simmer for a few minutes until leek and onion have softened but have not lost colour. Whisk in cold butter cubes, little by little, over medium heat to "mount" the sauce.

Arctic char

6 fillets of Arctic char,
   5-6 ounces each
flour seasoned with a little
   salt and pepper
1 tbsp oil
1 tbsp butter
maple-balsamic glaze
   (see page 36)

Dust fish lightly in seasoned flour. Heat oil and butter in pan. Brown fish on both sides and then transfer to 375°F oven for 5 minutes. Brush top side of fish with maple-balsamic glaze.

To serve:

Place a mound of warm parsnip purée in the centre of each plate. Present Arctic char on top of purée garnished with a few fresh grapefruit segments and nap grapefruit sauce around.

Steamed spinach, leeks or bok choy would be delicious accompaniments.

Maple Sugar-cured Gravlax

1 side of cured salmon (approximately 12 portions)

Gravlax means salmon ("lax") in a grave ("grav") and refers to the traditional Scandanavian way gravlax would be made: by first applying a salt cure and then weighting the salmon down by placing it underground. Here we use grated maple sugar and grainy mustard made with beer from the St. Ambroise microbrewery, as well as salt and dill to cure the fish.

1 side of Atlantic
salmon
½ cup coarse salt
4 tbsp coarsely ground
black pepper
½ cup maple sugar or
brown sugar
½ jar St. Ambroise
mustard or other grainy
mustard
½ cup chopped fresh
dill

Sprinkle salt, pepper and grated maple sugar onto flesh side of salmon.

Paste on mustard and add chopped dill. Cover with plastic wrap. Place on a baking pan or in a shallow dish with sides at least ½″ high to catch juices which will weep out.

Place a board and a weight over salmon and refrigerate for 3 days.

To serve:

Slice thinly with a sharp knife and present with Mustard Dill Mayonnaise on the side (see recipe on next page).

Mustard Dill Mayonnaise

Yield: 1 cup

2 egg yolks
1 tbsp Dijon mustard
1 tbsp grainy mustard
2 tbsp fresh lemon juice
1 cup vegetable oil
1 tbsp chopped fresh dill
salt & pepper

Place egg yolks, mustards and lemon juice in bowl of food processor and pulse until combined. With motor running, add oil in a slow, steady stream and continue to process until mayonnaise has thickened. Add dill and season as necessary.

Maple Syrup Pudding "Chômeur"

6 shallow ramekins

This is a traditional Québecois baked dessert literally meaning "pudding of the unemployed" – in other words a filling and economical dish because it was made with home-produced maple syrup. But it is also a delicious dessert whose batter cooks through the maple syrup, producing a fragrant, moist, pudding-like cake with a maple syrup sauce, usually served with light cream or milk.

2 oz butter for ramekins	Generously butter six 6-ounce ramekins.
1 cup flour 1½ tsp baking powder ½ tsp salt 1 beaten egg ⅓ cup milk 1 tbsp butter ½ cup sugar	Combine dry ingredients. Combine egg and milk. Cream together 1 tablespoon butter and sugar until light and fluffy. Add dry ingredients to the butter and sugar mixutre alternately with wet ingredients, starting and ending with dry ingredients. Mix until just combined.
1½ cups maple syrup 3 tbsp butter	Place a small scoop (2 ounces) of batter into each ramekin. For each ramekin, pour 4 tablespoons of maple syrup over batter and dot with ½ tablespoon of butter.

Bake at 350°F until golden and pudding springs back when pressed lightly, approximately 12 minutes.

Serve with light cream.

[Handwritten notes: boil 2c. wh cream, 2c m syrup, pour into pan, combine 3⅓ flour, 4 t. b. powder, 1½ t. salt, cream & butter 1c u. butter m temp; ⅔ c. br sugar, 4 eggs – beat in, 1½ c. milk – beat in, 2 t vanilla, add flour mixture; 400° 13x9"]

Searing Québec foie gras on a cast iron grill pan

Simmering rhubarb-rosemary compote

Wild Arctic char served on parsnip purée
with pink grapefruit and ginger jus

Facing page: Making gravlax with maple
sugar and St. Ambroise mustard

Sap drips from one of our sugar maples;
maple syrup pudding chômeur with pouring cream

April

After heartbreaking starts and stops, spring is now beginning to truly prevail over winter. The earth, exposed under the receding snow, is lined with a crazy maze of vole tracks and brightening mosses; a swollen stream of spring runoff races full force out of the edge of our woodland and the sun-warmed earth seems to heave a sigh, giving off the deep organic smell of spring itself.

Time to take down the birdfeeders and sweep off the porch that wraps around our dining room. Time to clear the land of the debris left after a long winter and time to scrub and set out our outside tables and chairs – of course it is still a little too cool to sit out but the mere look of them sets us to thinking about glasses of rosé to come…

In the gardens around the restaurant, reawakened bulbs push up shoots. Over the coming weeks snowdrops, periwinkle, crocuses and bluebells will give way to forget-me-nots, daffodils, forsythia, apple blossom, tulips and lilacs and then eventually to our reemerging perennials.

At the same time, in our surrounding maple and birch woodland, almost every day brings new surprises. It is in early spring, for a short time only before the canopy of leaves emerges, that sunlight can stream right through the woods to reach the forest floor. This warming, nourishing sunlight unleashes a furious succession of spring "ephemerals" – hepatica, wild leeks, dog tooth lilies, wood anemone, bloodroot, lilies-of-the-valley, fiddleheads, Jack-in-the-pulpits, Dutchmen's britches, maidenhair ferns and trilliums. It is almost as if the forest floor is a clock measuring out each minute advance of the season with the unfurling of every new wildflower and fern.

This leafless time also lets us see into and through the woodland in a way one cannot later on. A skein of spider webbing between bare branches catching the droplets and light left after an April shower is exquisite…bird watching is rarely so rewarding as when the objects of our desire can not so easily hide amongst the leaves…

There is a moment, sometime around the middle of April, when we are suddenly aware that the morning air is full of outrageously loud, beautiful birdsong and airborne avian antics designed for courtship. There is noisy roosting in leafless trees and rhythmic tapping as woodpeckers mark out their territory and prepare for nesting. After the isolated bird calls of winter the loudness of the chorus astonishes. Waves of migrating birds are passing through the region with each new warm front – not the least of which will be the Canada geese that will first appear as a fine inkline far off in the southern sky. They will then announce themselves more and more loudly as they pass overhead in their honking, jagged V formation, using the now ice-free Gatineau River to chart a course northward towards breeding grounds. The sight and sound of the returning geese evokes a deeply felt sense of reassurance, continuity and renewal.

By month's end the Hills are cloaked in a light green haze as pine and maple buds swell in unison. Trilliums carpet the forest floor behind the restaurant like snow. Daylight and warmth hold on into the evening. Frogs join the birds in mating evensong.

Inside we are still waiting for the return of another migratory species – our fair weather guests! Although the drive to Les Fougères is easy, the winter months seem to discourage some people from visiting. Too bad – it is so cozy and beautiful and delicious to be here in the snow! By the end of April however, people are moving again. We are looking forward to their return. Easter marks the beginning of a new busier season for us and we are occupied with organizing summer staffing and schedules, building inventory for the Store and calling down the "Spirit of the New Summer Menu"…

Salad Fougères

6 servings

This is a salad of greens tossed with hot sautéed lardons of smoked bacon and fresh goat's cheese from Ferme Floralpe in nearby Papineauville. The cheese gives a nice creamy counterpoint texturally to the crispiness of the greens and sautéed lardons and also delivers the distinctive tang of goat's cheese. A drizzle of hot and delicious bacon fat on the salad just before it is served is essential. We have had this salad on our menu since we opened Les Fougères in 1993 (and before that at our former restaurant "Loons" in the Beaches area of Toronto) because it is so delicious and popular. We will often make this into a main course salad by topping it with a softly boiled egg and adding slices of avocado, red onion and caramelized garlic.

8 cups mixed salad greens
6 ounces smoked bacon
   side
6 ounces fresh goat's cheese

Vinaigrette

$\frac{1}{4}$ cup Dijon mustard
$\frac{1}{4}$ cup red wine vinegar
1 cup vegetable oil
salt and pepper

Whisk together mustard and vinegar. Slowly add oil, whisking gently all the while. Season to taste.

To prepare salad:

Slice bacon into lardons (cubes) and sauté until golden and crispy. Toss salad with enough vinaigrette to coat leaves lightly. Divide salad between 6 bowls. Garnish with goat cheese, sautéed lardon bacon and a spoonful of the hot fat rendered from the lardons.

Parmesan-Crusted Davis Strait Halibut
with a Softly Poached Egg

6 servings

In springtime in particular, the northern halibut (sometimes called Greenland halibut or Baffin Island turbot) move to spawning grounds in the Davis Strait between Baffin Island and Greenland. This lovely white-fleshed fish is patted with parmesan bread-crumbs to make a delicious savoury crust. The softly poached egg yolk creates a luscious sauce for the dish. Serve the fish with asparagus at this time of year or sliced garden tomatoes and fresh basil later in the growing season when tomatoes have great flavour and acidity.

6 boneless fresh halibut steaks (5 ounces each)

$\frac{1}{2}$ loaf of white bread

2 cups grated Parmigiano Reggiano

zest of 1 lemon

$\frac{3}{4}$ cup melted butter

salt and pepper to taste

6 eggs

lemon zest, olive oil, shaved Parmigiano Reggiano and balsamic vinegar as garnish

sprinkle of fleur de sel and ground black pepper

Pulse fresh bread slices in processor. Place in a large bowl and add grated Parmigiano, lemon zest, butter, salt and pepper and mix gently.

Pat crust mixture liberally onto halibut portions and place on a buttered baking sheet. Place in 400°F oven for 10 minutes or until crust is golden and fish is cooked.

Break eggs into boiling water which has $\frac{1}{4}$ cup white vinegar added to it. When the water returns to the boil, remove the pot from the heat and let the eggs sit in the water for another 2 minutes.

To serve:

Place cooked, crusted halibut on a warm plate. Remove the softly cooked egg from the water with a slotted spoon. Place carefully on the halibut crust.

Garnish the fish with shaves of Parmigiano Reggiano, lemon zest, olive oil, balsamic vinegar, fleur de sel and freshly cracked black peppercorns.

Maple Syrup Pie with Crème Fraîche

Makes one 12" tart

This is another celebration of freshly tapped and boiled local maple syrup. This recipe involves reducing maple syrup and breadcrumbs and produces an intense maple syrup experience akin to eating maple syrup taffy off the snow as a child.

Filling

3 cups maple syrup
3 cups fresh white
   breadcrumbs

Stir maple syrup and fresh breadcrumbs together in a pot. Simmer until bubbling and reduced to a taffy-like consistency.

Pastry

2 cups flour
1 cup chopped cold butter
pinch salt
approx $\frac{2}{3}$ cup ice water

In processor, pulse flour with cold butter and salt. Add just enough water to bring the pastry together. Chill. Roll out dough and fit it into a 12″ tart pan (preferably with a removable bottom). Chill again. Prick with a fork. Bake in a 350°F oven until golden. Cool.

Crème fraîche

1 cup whipping cream
1 cup sour cream

Stir together the cream and the sour cream. Leave loosely covered at room temperature overnight. Stir and refrigerate.

To assemble:

Pour syrup mixture into baked, cooled pastry shell. Bake at 350°F until bubbling all over. Remove from oven and cool completely. When set, cut into neat slices and serve with crème fraîche.

Making Salad Fougères

Crumbling goat's cheese over dressed greens

Sautéed lardon bacon hot from the pan

Vinaigrettes

Eliette delivering her artisanal goat cheese from
Ferme Floralpe in nearby Papineauville

The forest is still bare, the new lilac leaves are just days old, but the daffodils are already in full bloom

Wild leeks, trilliums and anemones pushing through the carpet of last year's leaves on the forest floor

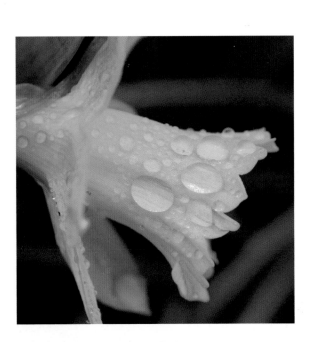

Parmesan crusted halibut with a softly poached egg on spring asparagus

Maple syrup pie

May

On an early May morning the world around us is like a pointillist painting. Lime green buttons of bud dot each and every branch in our back woods and the forest floor is scattered with white and the occasional deep purple trillium at their peak. Sunlight is streaming through the woods and the air is warm.

By the time we have finished serving lunch we realize there are no more dots – fragile new leaves have begun to emerge from buds. Within only a day or two these leaves will have stretched out to form a canopy over the top of the woodland and the showy succession of spring woodland flowers will be replaced by the understated beauty of shade loving ferns, mosses, mycelium and other more discreet woodland flora. The alchemy of decay to regeneration, which is occurring under every footfall in the woods, silently, but insistently, continues.

Over the coming days the trilliums will become increasingly blousy and tinged with pink. They will soon die back into their rootstock, dormant again until next spring.

In the gardens at Les Fougères the attention of the eye has shifted from forest floor trilliums to the candy store colours of muscari, forget-me-nots, daffodils and opening tulips in the planted garden. Easter was a turning point towards spring and busier times ahead but it is really Mother's Day, the second Sunday in May, which marks for us the true gateway into the busy summer season. Our ramped-up summer schedule for servers, cooks and store personnel kicks in and we welcome on board new staff and student part-timers who will help us shoulder the summer workload. Mother's Day, our busiest day in terms of numbers of guests, is a daunting start for new employees, but ultimately gets us all into our stride.

Mother's Day means other things, too – the local wisdom is that hummingbird feeders must go up now because returning ruby-throated hummingbirds will create an attachment to feeders as soon as they arrive, which is anytime now. We have many hummingbird feeders around the restaurant, close to windows and outside tables. The world seems to stop and hold its breath at the sight of these iridescent, almost weightless jewels hovering and dipping, hovering and dipping into the feeders after their epic migratory return from Mexico and points beyond.

May also brings something else – blackflies and mosquitoes! We install screens on our wrap-around verandah creating an outside oasis protected from bugs. But the return of the insects also means that ants are helping to ease open peony heads, blossoms are being pollinated, butterflies return and generally the delicate, intricate and productive interplay and dependency between plants and insects is set into motion again.

This is also the time when we cut the lawn for the first time. The mowing releases one of the first real scents of summer. This reacquaintance with the sweet fragrance of freshly cut grass stirs not only our noses but also our feelings, making thoughts flood back of summers gone by.

The soil in our vegetable and flower beds is being turned and fed with compost and all seems ready for planting out our seedlings. It is a game of chance and daring at this time though – a night frost is not impossible or improbable and we try to resist the temptation of planting out before the end of the month.

Towards the end of May we present the new summer menu to all staff. We are always working on the next menu and we have been working on this one for months. This menu hopefully captures the tastes, aromas, colours and textures of the main growing season of this northern country. The staff help us refine the recipes and plate presentations, and dip into the wine cellar to discuss best wine matches. Background notes explaining the whys and hows of each menu item are distributed and discussed. For us internally this is a moment of disassembling and reassembling and we come out of it sometimes bruised, but bandaged and always better thanks to everyone's input. We are all primed and ready for what we are about to do together in the kitchens, dining room, store, gardens, and behind the scenes in the office and cellar. This is a truly exciting moment. We are like racehorses ready for the starting gun. Mother's Day is it and we're off!

By the end of the month we are beginning to harvest early edible flowers and herbs such as Johnny-jump-ups, salad burnett, chervil, sorrel, chives and early salad greens. In the kitchen we are also enjoying the fleeting pleasures of fiddleheads, asparagus, morels and wild leeks. Outside, the bright yellow forsythia bushes have faded but bleeding hearts and apple blossom are still holding forth and the lilacs have just begun to bloom. In that last week of May, we notice, for the first time, that the evening air is full of perfume. Summer is surely on its way.

Maple Roasted Almonds with Fleur de Sel

1 pound, approximately 8 cocktail-size servings

These almonds are a great favourite in our store where we sell them by the jar – perfect for before dinner drinks. We also love offering them with cheeses. The interplay of nuttiness, saltiness and maple sweetness is delicious. Fleur de sel is the "flower" of salt which forms on top of evaporating sea water. It is hand-harvested with special rakes from salt pans built to collect tidal water. Its delicate mineral and briny character is one of Mother Nature's purest gifts.

1 pound almonds, skin on
$\frac{1}{3}$ cup maple syrup
1 tbsp vegetable oil
Fleur de sel to taste

Toss almonds with maple syrup. Add oil last and toss to coat.

Spread on parchment-lined baking sheet and bake at 325°F until fragrant and syrup has thickened and coated the nuts, about 20 minutes, stirring every 5 minutes. Remove from oven and sprinkle with salt while almonds are warm and sticky.

Let cool on pan. Break apart any clumps and package in jars. Store airtight at room temperature.

Asparagus, Fiddleheads and Morels with a Soft Poached Egg

4 portions

Asparagus, fiddleheads and morels, all native to this region, impatiently push up and out of the spring soil at about the same time of year. The deep woodsy flavour of the honey-combed morel and the bracing stored-up vitality of asparagus and fiddleheads partner naturally. The rich sauce-producing egg yolk and the inimitable nuttiness and natural salt of Parmigiano Reggiano and pancetta also make this a distinctive Spring treat. That a fiddlehead is an unfurled fern (fougère) also means that using fiddleheads in springtime has a special significance to us here at Les Fougères.

20 asparagus spears
16 fiddleheads, well
   cleaned
$\frac{1}{3}$ cup butter
8 fresh morels, sliced in
   quarters lengthwise
8 slices pancetta
4 eggs
$\frac{1}{4}$ cup white vinegar
a 4-ounce piece of
   Parmigiano Reggiano
extra-virgin olive oil
aged balsamic vinegar
fleur de sel and freshly
   ground black pepper

Steam asparagus and fiddleheads until tender. Toss in butter and season with a little salt and pepper.

Render pancetta slices in a pan with a little olive oil until crisped. Remove pancetta slices and reserve. Add sliced morels to pan with rendered pancetta fat and sauté until mushrooms are thoroughly cooked.

Bring 2 litres of water to a rapid boil in a saucepan. Add white vinegar to the water. Carefully break the eggs into the water. When water returns to a boil, turn off the heat and let the eggs sit in the water for 2 minutes. Strain the softly poached eggs out of the water with a slotted spoon.

To serve:

Arrange hot asparagus, fiddleheads and morels on 4 plates. Place an egg on top of each, then garnish with shavings of Parmigiano Reggiano, the crisped pancetta slices, a drizzle of extra-virgin olive oil and aged balsamic vinegar. Garnish with a sprinkling of fleur de sel and freshly ground black pepper to taste.

Sautéed Veal Sweetbreads and Pancetta
on Orecchiette with Peas, Mint and Red Onion

Makes 4 servings

Veal sweetbreads, particularly the "pommes", or those from the thymus gland of calves, are delicate in flavour and texture. Here they are sautéed in rendered pancetta fat and finished with balsamic vinegar, good stock and white wine so they have a glazed outside and creamy inside – delicious, especially when they are partnered with peas, mint, red onion and pancetta in a stock and wine reduction which is caught in the hollow of orecchiette pasta's "little ears".

Orecchiette pasta with peas, mint and red onion

4 cups chicken stock
2 cups white wine
$\frac{1}{2}$ cup unsalted butter
$\frac{1}{2}$ cup thinly sliced red onion
$\frac{3}{4}$ cup frozen peas
3 tbsp chopped fresh mint
4 cups cooked orecchiette pasta
salt and freshly cracked black pepper

Place stock and wine in a sauté pan, bring to a boil then reduce heat and simmer to reduce by half. Add butter, red onion and peas and swirl pan over low heat until butter has been incorporated into the sauce and the red onion is tender. Toss the chopped mint and cooked orecchiette pasta into the sauce and season with sea salt and freshly cracked black pepper.

Glazed sweetbreads

1½ pounds veal "pomme" sweetbreads

4 bay leaves

1 tsp black peppercorns

2 sprigs of fresh thyme

1 leek, white part only, chopped and rinsed well

1 stick of celery, chopped

1 carrot, chopped

juice of 1 lemon

1 onion, chopped

8 slices pancetta

1 tbsp olive oil

1 tbsp butter

flour for dusting sweetbreads

1 red onion, sliced

1 clove of garlic, crushed

½ cup aged balsamic vinegar

½ cup white wine

½ cup chicken stock

Rinse sweetbreads. Cover with cold water and add bay leaves, peppercorns, thyme, chopped onion, leek, celery, carrot and lemon juice. Bring to boil over high heat, then reduce heat to medium and simmer for a few minutes. Strain and refresh sweetbreads in cold water. When cool enough to handle, peel off membrane. Place in a colander over a bowl and cover with a 2 lb weight (such as a stack of plates). Refrigerate for at least 2 hours.

Slice sweetbreads into ½″ medallions. Render pancetta in saucepan with olive oil and butter. Remove and reserve pancetta. Lightly dust sweetbreads with flour, season with salt and pepper and add to hot pancetta fat in pan to brown. Add red onion and garlic and cook until sweetbreads are golden brown and crispy on all sides and onion is softened. Pour off excess fat from the pan and deglaze with balsamic vinegar, wine and stock. Reduce liquid to a glaze while turning sweetbreads to coat.

To serve:

Place sauced pasta in a shallow bowl. Place glazed sweetbreads on pasta and top with crisped pancetta. Garnish with fresh thyme, mint and lemon zest.

Lia's Godmother's Spring Rhubarb Coffee Cake

Makes one 9" x 12" cake

Lia Turcotte is one of our Pastry Chefs. She kindly agreed to share this favourite family recipe with us.

2 cups flour
1 teaspoon baking soda
$\frac{1}{4}$ teaspoon salt
$1\frac{1}{2}$ cups packed brown
   sugar
$\frac{1}{2}$ cup vegetable oil
1 egg
1 cup milk
1 tablespoon vanilla extract
$2\frac{1}{2}$ cups rhubarb cut into
   1-inch chunks

Topping
$\frac{1}{2}$ cup granulated sugar
1 teaspoon ground ginger

Combine flour, baking soda and salt. Mix in brown sugar.

In a separate bowl, whisk together eggs, milk and vanilla and add to dry ingredients. Whisk in oil in a steady stream. Stir in rhubarb chunks.

Combine sugar and ginger for topping. Spread batter into a greased 9″ by 12″ baking pan and sprinkle with topping. Bake at 350°F for approximately 40 minutes, or until the cake springs back to the touch. Garnish with fresh poached rhubarb.

Asparagus, fiddleheads and morels with a softly poached egg, pancetta and Parmigiano Reggiano

Previous page: The garden is waking up; trilliums along the woodland trail

Spring at Table 11

Sautéed veal sweetbreads and pancetta on orrechietti with peas and mint

Johnny jump-ups return to the kitchen

Staff tasting the new menu and discussing wine pairings
(it's a hard job but someone's got to do it)

Screens are up and the verandah is ready to go

Lia's godmother's spring rhubarb coffee cake

Québec artisanal cheeses, clockwise from left: Heidi, Peter, Gré des Champs, Mi-Carême, Peau Rouge, Sieur Corbeau and Cendré des Prés and maple roasted almonds with fleur de sel

June

Leaving the restaurant one night in early June, we are thrilled by the company of phosphorescent silver green pin lights pulsing here and there in the woods around us. The fireflies have suddenly arrived and their appearance makes us realize that we have been expecting them in the same way that we anticipated the return of the Canada Geese earlier in spring. The crazy, darting midnight dancing of the fireflies makes us feel more like live wires too.

The gardens are filling in with leaf and bloom as the perennials take centre stage. The last days of lilac are upon us and those dining on our porch will miss being caught up in its fragrant breezes. But, embarrassment of riches – honeysuckle, wild phlox, and spikes of lupins take up the mantle – and then what conjures up the glory days of June more than the heady scent, graduated rich colours and opulent blossom of peonies? Peonies in the garden or as a cut flower are a royal grace note in life, transforming the very feel of the space and time they occupy. We always feel so lucky to be able to surround guests with perfumed armfuls of peonies from the garden and know that we all become more elegant in their reflected presence.

On every dining room table small vases of airy euphorbia, daisies and small peony heads are one way we like to say a personal welcome to each guest.

In the woodland the maidenhair fern has unfurled itself into graceful dentelle work along circular arcs of slender dark lacquered stems. It was this delicate fern that drew us to call our restaurant "Les Fougères" (which means "the ferns" in French). On a June day, many years ago now, on one of our many visits to the property as we tried to gather resources to buy it, we walked in the woods and every step we took was brushed with this extraordinary fern. We were very affected by its beauty and said to each other if we ever were able to buy the property that we would call it "Les Fougères". A year later in 1993 we were the thrilled and terrified new owners of a sylvan dream.

Another incredible plant, now in bloom, is a woodland orchid – the yellow ladyslipper. These pendulous moccasins of gold have found a place in the woods behind us where the shadow is dappled with just enough light for them to flourish. Coming upon this glade of slippers in bloom is breathtaking. Revealing the location of this rare glade was an unforgettably beautiful gift given to us from Helmut and Rita, the previous owners of the Les Fougères property, for which we will always be thankful. Along with other native treasures, we have moved several ladyslipper plants close to our woodland trail where they can be seen and they seem to be taking. Our woodland trail is a portal into the edge of the woods which stands as an invitation to experience, even in its short span, a soaring overhead natural cathedral and a forest floor underfoot of extraordinary beauty.

June is the month when we really start using our gardens and local farm produce in earnest. We receive local produce almost daily and all cooks begin to take up the habit of the pre-service walk in our gardens to gather salad greens, herbs and edible flowers. These tender shoots and blooms only survive a few hours once cut so picking them is generally the last thing done before lunch or dinner. This walk is very good for the soul, too, after the rigours of making sure your station is invincibly prepped before the intensity of service hits.

Being busy again after those calmer winter months is a great adrenaline rush and those who stay in this profession thrive on the pressure. Of course, there is always a real sense of satisfaction derived from doing something you are passionate about, especially if it makes others happy. Everything comes into play: knowledge, menu, ingredients, technique, teamwork, hard work, attention to detail, speed, creativity, devotion and pride. Topping the sense of individual satisfaction, though, is the exhilaration felt when the intersecting efforts of the whole team – kitchen, dining room, office and gardens –

come respectfully and supportively together to create an oasis of gastronomy and hospitality (even if behind the scenes it sometimes seems like we are passing through a tornado!). At our best, a good "service" is a bit like ballet in its focused discipline, minutely rehearsed movements and intricate, interdependent relationships between front and back of the house and everything in between. For all our differences, everyone who stays as part of the team at Les Fougères is passionate and driven. Soul is bared in the work and we all want to help create something special – that makes all the difference and all our various efforts intersect at every turn.

Towards the end of June we reach summer solstice: our longest day and shortest night. The earth responds and we are surrounded by roses, iris, daisies, black-eyed Susans, poppies, bachelor's buttons, calendula and nasturtiums. Bird mating and nest-building are for the most part over and soon there will be fledglings.

The air has been heating up and June will often offer the first thirty-plus degree heat wave followed by what seems to be the thunderstorm to end all thunderstorms. We awake to find the atmosphere cleared but our precious peonies with their heavy regal heads dashed to the ground. All part of the cycle but also a reminder to notice and celebrate what we have when we have it.

Vinaigrettes

While there are many times when one yearns simply for good aged balsamic vinegar and/or a luscious extra-virgin olive oil as a salad dressing, we also find lots of room in our hearts and on our plates for prepared vinaigrettes. The following vinaigrettes use good Dijon mustard to liaise between oil and vinegar and seasonal bounty such as fruits and herbs to produce dressings which are fabulous with salad greens and grilled vegetables, and even as a marinade for meats heading to the barbecue.

Classic vinaigrette

3 tbsp Dijon mustard
$\frac{1}{4}$ cup red wine vinegar
1 cup vegetable oil
salt and pepper

Whisk together mustard and vinegar. Slowly add oil, whisking gently all the while. Season to taste.

Raspberry or cassis vinaigrette

Whisk $\frac{1}{2}$ cup homemade raspberry or blackcurrant jam into 1 cup Classic vinaigrette.

Pesto vinaigrette

Process 2 cups clean basil leaves with $\frac{1}{4}$ cup pine nuts, $\frac{1}{4}$ cup Parmigiano Reggiano and $\frac{2}{3}$ cup good extra-virgin olive oil. Season to taste. Add this to 1 cup Classic vinaigrette and whisk.

Maple Pommery vinaigrette

Add $\frac{1}{2}$ cup maple syrup and $\frac{1}{2}$ cup grainy Pommery mustard to 1 cup Classic Vinaigrette and whisk.

Red pepper chèvre vinaigrette

Skin, seed and chop 3 roasted red peppers. Briefly process peppers with $\frac{1}{2}$ cup goat's cheese and 1 cup Classic Vinaigrette in food processor or blender. Season to taste.

Hoisin-marmalade vinaigrette

Briefly process 1 cup Classic Vinaigrette with $\frac{1}{4}$ cup hoisin sauce, $\frac{1}{4}$ cup Seville orange marmalade and $\frac{1}{2}$ cup fresh coriander leaves. Season to taste. Thin with orange juice if a thinner consistency is desired.

Partridgeberry vinaigrette

1 tsp butter
1 tsp olive oil
1 small red onion,
   sliced
$\frac{1}{4}$ cup red currant jelly
2 tbsp balsamic vinegar
2 tbsp port
2 tbsp Dijon mustard
1 cup partridgeberries
1 tsp each orange and
   lemon zest
fresh thyme

Heat the oil and butter in a heavy saucepan. Add the red onion slices and soften them gently. Whisk in jelly, vinegar, port and mustard and bring to a boil. Stir in berries, zest and thyme and return to a boil. Remove from heat and let cool.

Whisk together with 1 cup Classic Vinaigrette.

Wild Mushroom Soup

6 servings

One of our most popular soups. Using dried as well as fresh wild mushrooms ensures a depth of earthy, haunting mushroominess because the flavour is so concentrated and strong in the dried mushroom. Dried ceps deliver the most intense flavour. We are fortunate that most of the very best wild mushrooms are native to our region. Depending on the time of the season we will use locally picked morels, ceps and/or chanterelles. We also add portobellos and oyster mushrooms when supplies of the fleeting wild mushrooms are limited.

2 cups dried cep or
   porcini mushrooms
4 tbsp butter
1 onion, finely chopped
1 pound fresh wild
   mushrooms such as
   morels, ceps or
   chanterelles, chopped
1 potato, peeled and
   chopped
3 cups chicken stock
2 cloves of garlic, minced
2 tbsp fresh tarragon,
   chopped
½ cup whipping cream,
   if desired
½ cup medium-dry sherry
lemon zest and white
   truffle oil for garnish
salt and pepper to taste

Cover dried wild mushrooms with boiling water and let stand for at least a half hour. Remove, chop and reserve rehydrated mushrooms. Pass soaking liquid ("mushroom liquor") through a fine sieve to remove any sand and reserve.

Sweat onions gently in butter over medium heat until soft and translucent. Add chopped fresh and rehydrated mushrooms and garlic and sauté for several minutes. Reserve a little of this mixture to garnish the soup at the end. Add potato, stock, reserved mushroom liquor and sherry and simmer until potato is soft. Purée in food processor. Add tarragon. Add cream if desired and adjust seasoning to taste. Bring back to a boil and serve garnished with lemon zest, fresh thyme, white truffle oil and reserved sautéed mushroom pieces.

Lamb Sausages
with Roasted Red Pepper, Mint, Orange and Goat's Cheese

12 sausages

Making sausages which are juicy but not fatty, don't split while being filled or on the grill, are memorably tasty, aren't crumbly, only have good natural ingredients and no filler is a labour of love which has occupied Charlie for decades. Charlie makes several kinds of sausages, especially in summer for the barbecue, which sell like hotcakes in the store and also enhance the restaurant menus. This recipe is for one of the most popular sausages at Les Fougères. Using these sausages in a pasta with homemade tomato sauce, a touch of Pernod and braised fennel would also be delicious.

2 pounds chilled coarsely ground lamb (medium fat i.e. from the shoulder)

3 cloves garlic, chopped

1 orange, seeded and finely chopped

2 red peppers, roasted, skinned and chopped

1 tbsp fennel seed

1 bunch Italian parsley, chopped

2 tbsp chopped fresh mint

2 tbsp chopped fresh tarragon

1 tsp sugar

1 tsp sambal oelek or other hot chilli paste

salt and pepper

½ cup balsamic vinegar

½ cup goat's cheese, crumbled

sausage casings

Mix together all sausage ingredients (except casings) until well combined and refrigerate for 2 hours or until completely cold.

Soak sausage casings in water for 20 minutes, then rinse well.

Fit casings onto sausage maker. Fill sausage. Form into 5-inch links by twisting, then cut between sausages to separate.

Barbecue over medium heat, turning to brown all sides, until cooked through and juices run clear when sausages are pierced.

Strawberry and Rose Geranium Sorbet

6 servings

Summer has arrived and big bold sorbets full of the flavours of the season sing out the possibilities of the farm and garden. Other summer sorbet favourites are dark chocolate and garden mint, blackcurrant and lemon thyme, gooseberry and honey, and lemon verbena with Earl Grey. A tuile buscuit cup is a lovely way to present this dessert, surrounded by fresh berries and edible flowers.

Sorbet

4 cups sliced strawberries,
    preferably just picked
$\frac{3}{4}$ cup sugar
juice of $\frac{1}{2}$ lemon
handful of rose geranium
    leaves

Simmer all ingredients together until fruit is soft, sugar has completely dissolved and mixture is fragrant with rose geranium.

Strain through a sieve, pressing well on solids. Discard solids.

Place mixture in an ice cream maker and proceed according to manufacturer's instructions.

Tuile biscuit cup

2 ounces sugar
2 ounces melted butter
2 ounces flour
2 egg whites
$\frac{1}{2}$ tsp real vanilla essence

Mix ingredients together until completely smooth. Spread in thin 4″ rounds on a Silpat or parchment-lined baking tray. Place in a 350°F oven until the tuiles are beginning to turn golden brown, about 4 minutes. Remove from oven and, using a metal spatula, transfer each round from the baking tray onto an upturned empty water glass so that the edges of the still pliable disk fall over the edges of the upturned glass. Work quickly because the cookies cool and harden almost immediately! Pinch the edges of the tuile at regular intervals to create a "frill". Remove from the glass and turn upside to form a cup.

If you wish to create a cobweb design embedded in the tuile, reserve some of the above tuile mixture and add some melted dark chocolate to it. Place this in a squeeze bottle. Before placing the baking tray in the oven squeeze circles of chocolate mixture onto each plain tuile. Pull a wooden skewer through the circles to create a cobweb design. Bake and form as above.

Wild mushroom soup with chanterelles,
ceps, King Eryngii mushrooms and
fresh lemon thyme from the garden

Christophe of Champignons Le Coprin
delivering some of his mushrooms

Clockwise from top: A ray of sunlight reveals ladyslippers; the woodland path behind Les Fougères; maidenhair ferns that gave the restaurant its name

Previous page: Making lamb sausages

Strawberry geranium sorbet with
rose geranium leaves from our garden

Supplier Louis Audet arrives
with local strawberries

FRAISES
de l'Ontario

July

Neighbouring farms and our own gardens are now in full swing, providing the kitchen with lettuces, tender chards and greens, herbs and baby vegetables and each table and window bay with daily picked blooms. Sun-ripened gooseberries and red and black currants are now ready for picking and we try to beat the crows to the harvest. Edible summer flowers such as calendula, Johnny-jump-ups, fuschia, begonia, bachelor's buttons, borage, nasturtiums, mallow, lavender, marigolds, rose petals, herb flowers and pansies help our dishes exclaim "summer"!

And then come the mushrooms…chanterelles and ceps first before it gets too hot and especially if we have had a bit of rain. When the chanterelle and raspberry seasons peak at the same time Heaven's kitchen door seems to swing open. The tart sweetness of local raspberries and lemon thyme from the garden paired with earthy but somehow champagne-kissed chanterelles, especially when the backdrop is slow roasted, moist, Red Bro chicken (raised especially for us by La Ferme aux Saveurs des Monts on a feed of alfalfa and corn) is indeed heaven-sent. The counterpoints in textures, sweetness and acidity between these fleeting seasonal gifts dignify our culinary calendar.

And the garden continues to mark time more precisely than we could ever imagine. July began with peonies, baptisia and penstemon but now is graced with stands of delphinium, hollyhocks, clematis, day lilies, astilbe, roses and poppies. With guilt we harvest zucchini flowers and impossibly tiny and tender patty pan squashes. Early tomatoes are ripening as well as early seeded beets, carrots, snowpeas, radishes and chards.

The insistent heat of mid summer fills the days of late July as does the continuous drone of cicadas and huge beautiful dragonflies cutting this way and that above the gardens. When we look up into the velvet night sky we catch and then lose sight of bats in their crazy staccato pirouetting, the moonlight catching a wing for a second before they seem to disappear on a knife's edge into the warm night air again.

Chilled Tomato and Yogurt Soup
with Matane Shrimp, Basil, Mint and Coriander

8 servings

A lovely tangy summer soup, full of layers of kitchen garden flavours and garnished with the tiny sweet cold-water shrimp of the St. Lawrence estuary.

26 ounces fresh or tinned skinless, seedless tomatoes

2 English cucumbers

3 cups plain yogurt

1 tsp curry powder (see page 96)

$\frac{1}{4}$ cup extra-virgin olive oil

1 cup fresh basil leaves, lightly packed

1 cup fresh mint leaves, lightly packed

$\frac{1}{2}$ cup fresh coriander leaves, lightly packed

salt and pepper to taste

1 cup cooked Matane shrimp

yogurt for garnish

Place tomatoes and cucumbers in a food processor and purée until smooth. Add yogurt, olive oil, curry powder and fresh herbs. Continue to process until smooth. Season to taste with salt and pepper, then refrigerate until very cold.

Serve cold, garnished with a little plain yogurt and some Matane shrimps.

July

Grainfed Chicken Breast from La Ferme aux Saveurs des Monts with Mi-Carême, Chanterelles, Raspberries and Lemon Thyme

6 servings

As long as we have a good bit of rain this month, the golden glades and earthy yet acidic scent of chanterelles occur in the dappled light of the woodland edge. Locations of these glades are, understandably, heavily guarded secrets. We rely primarily on local foragers for our supply. This recipe is a showcase for the mushrooms and raspberries in season now and uses the beautiful grain-fed chicken from Val-des-Monts, which we are so lucky to have nearby. Mi-Carême, the oozing, Brie de Meaux-like cheese from Ile-aux-Grûes in Québec's Charlevoix region, adds superb, almost mushroomy depth itself. Lemon thyme, our favourite thyme, underscores the acidity in the raspberries and chanterelles. We grow lots of it in our gardens at Les Fougères.

2 tbsp olive oil
2 tbsp butter
6 grainfed chicken breasts
2 cups fresh chanterelle
  mushrooms, sliced if
  large
1 onion, diced
½ cup dry white wine
1 cup chicken stock
½ cup raspberry syrup
  (see below)
6 ounces Mi-Carême cheese,
  cut into 12 slices
fresh raspberries, lemon
  zest and fresh lemon
  thyme for garnish

Melt butter with olive oil in a large frying pan. Sear chicken breasts until golden on both sides. Transfer from pan to a baking sheet and place in a 375°F oven for 14 minutes to cook through completely.

Add chanterelles and onion to pan in which you have cooked the chicken and sauté gently until tender. Deglaze with white wine and stock, scraping up brown bits from bottom of pan. Remove chanterelles and keep warm. Add raspberry syrup to pan, bring to a boil and then reduce heat to medium and simmer to reduce to a loose glaze.

To serve:

Slice chicken breasts into three pieces each. Tuck a slice of Mi-Carême cheese between each piece of chicken and place on a plate. Nap glaze over top and finish with warm chanterelles, fresh raspberries and lemon thyme.

Yukon Gold potato purée with early sweetcorn stirred in and sautéed Toscano kale or patty pan squash would be delicious with this dish.

Raspberry syrup

1 cup raspberries
1 cup rice vinegar
$\frac{2}{3}$ cup sugar

Cover raspberries with vinegar in a ceramic bowl. Wrap well with plastic wrap and let sit at room temperature one week.

Pass through a sieve and discard solids. Pour vinegar mixture into heavy bottomed pot, add sugar and bring to a boil. Reduce heat and simmer until vinegar is concentrated and syrupy.

Pan-Fried Wild Pickerel with Gooseberries, Red Onion, Tarragon and Pancetta

6 servings

Gooseberries are so under-rated and not nearly available enough. We have several bushes and when the fruit is ripe we enjoy a week or two of the unique sharpness of the gooseberry in dessert and savoury preparations. Here, we partner it with the anise flavour of tarragon, red onion and nutty, salty pancetta in a distinctive, albeit simple sauce for the lovely sweet white flesh of wild Lake Winnipeg pickerel.

1 tbsp olive oil
1 tbsp butter
4 ounces sliced pancetta
4 pickerel fillets (6 ounces each)
flour seasoned with a little salt and pepper
1 cup white wine
1½ cups fish or chicken stock
¾ cup red onion, thinly sliced
¾ cup fresh ripe gooseberries
⅔ cup cold butter, cubed
2 tbsp fresh tarragon

In an oven-proof sauté pan over medium-high heat, gently render pancetta in butter and oil until crispy. Remove pancetta from pan and reserve.

Dust fillets lightly with seasoned flour and fry in the hot pancetta fat in pan for 2 minutes on one side. Turn over and place pan in 375°F oven for 6 minutes to finish cooking fish.

Remove fish from oven. Remove fish from pan and reserve. Add stock and white wine to pan and bring to boil over high heat until reduced by one third. Add red onion and gooseberries. Swirl in butter cubes, simmering gently until incorporated. Add chopped tarragon.

To serve:

Place a fish fillet on each plate, nap with gooseberry sauce and top with crisped pancetta. New potatoes and sautéed Swiss chard, zucchini or fine green beans would be lovely with this dish.

Pure Cassis Jellies

Approximately 4 dozen

This is a recipe that means a lot to us because it is so pure and brings out the black-currants' unique intensity. In a way, it is a guiding light for us culinarily – telling us not to play around with things too much and to use techniques which simply help ingredients shine with their own distinct character.

5 cups blackcurrants
juice of 1 lemon
sugar as required
fine sugar for coating

Purée blackcurrants in food processor until smooth. Stir in lemon juice.

Pass blackcurrant purée through a sieve or a fine food mill to remove seeds and skins.

Place strained purée in a heavy-bottomed pot. For each cup of strained purée, stir in $\frac{2}{3}$ cup sugar. Bring mixture to a boil over medium-high heat, stirring occasionally, then reduce heat to low and simmer, stirring often, until mixture gels, about 1 hour.

To check for gel, place a teaspoonful of purée onto a cold plate and refrigerate for 2 minutes until completely cold, or freeze for a few seconds. If purée holds together and can be peeled off the plate in one piece, jellies are ready.

Remove pot from heat and pour purée onto a 6″ x 8″ tray lined with a Silpat or parchment paper. The size of the tray will determine the thickness of the jellies – a smaller tray will give thicker jellies. Let sit at room temperature to cool completely and finish the gelling process, ideally overnight. Do not cover.

Run a knife around edges of tray, tip jelly out onto cutting board and cut into desired shapes. Roll in fine sugar and place on a cooling rack overnight to dry further. Again, do not cover. Store between layers of waxed paper in an airtight container.

Dark Chocolate Truffles

Approximately 24 truffles

19 oz bittersweet chocolate,
    chopped (1st amount)
2 cups whipping cream
1½ cups butter
2½ tbsp cognac
8 oz bittersweet chocolate,
    chopped (2nd amount)
½ cup good quality
    cocoa

Make ganache by placing first amount of chocolate, cream and butter in a metal bowl over simmering water. Warm gently, stirring occasionally, until chocolate has melted completely and ganache is smooth. Remove from heat and stir in cognac.

Refrigerate ganache until firm. Scoop mixture by the teaspoon and roll into balls.

While you are rolling the ganache, set second amount of chocolate in a bowl over hot water to melt completely. Remove from heat.

Dip ganache balls into chocolate, let the excess drip off, then immediately roll in cocoa.

Ripe green zebra tomatoes

Ripening cherry tomatoes

Chilled tomato-yogurt soup with
Matane shrimp, mint and coriander

Panfried pickerel with our gooseberries, red onion, tarragon and pancetta,
garnished with bachelor's button petals and borage flowers

PHOTO COURTESY LA FERME AUX SAVEURS DES MONTS

Sylvain raises grainfed chickens
at La Ferme aux Saveurs des Monts

Chicken breast with local wild chanterelles,
raspberries, Mi-Carême and lemon thyme

Head gardener Jenny Crawley creates
enchanted gardens at Les Fougères

Tjeerd of Bristol Farm
arrives with a rainbow of carrots

Fiona's woodland trail is an invitation to experience, even in its short span, a soaring overhead natural cathedral and a forest floor underfoot of extraordinary beauty.

Cutting pure cassis jellies

Mignardise plate with cassis jellies, truffles, candied pecans, biscuits and strawberries

Picking vegetables, lettuces, herbs and edible flowers
in the gardens before dinner service begins

Edible garnishes from our garden: Summer savoury, lemon verbena, opal basil, red currants, mesclun, lavender, bachelor button petals, calendula, Italian parsley, salad burnet, nasturtium flowers, Tip Top Alaska nasturtium leaves, sweet cicely, johnny jump-ups, dill, borage, sweet woodruff, scented geranium, mallow, mint, sage, lemon thyme, pansies, oregano, begonia, chive flowers

Simple summer perfection: Garden radishes on buttered bread with fleur de sel

August

The month of August holds two seasons. The first long weekend of August seems to crown the glory days of summer: gardens full of blooms at their peak; incessant heat which sometimes even ramps up overnight; clematis cresting the arbour and almost more summer produce than we have time to cook. Beautiful weddings are also unfolding in our woodland gardens.

Then one day in mid-August the wheel turns and the cooler evenings begin. At night we will stay out late, eyes towards the sky as August takes us through the meteorite shower season. The morning grass is lush with heavy dew as the cooler night air releases its moisture. The lilies, morning glories and hollyhocks begin to wane and glorious, pining sunflowers, asters, hellenium, echinacea, goldenrod and thistles become the dominant personalities in the perennial borders.

The kitchen gardens revel in being able to recoup in the cooler night air after a hot day and we can hardly keep up with the harvest – so many different varieties of tomatoes, beets and salad greens; an abundance of patty pan squashes AND the squashes that got away and have grown to ludicrous sizes. Sweet carrots, hot peppers, fennel, kohlrabi, beets, beans, peas, leeks, kale, chicory, rapini, cucumbers and more create an avalanche of gorgeous produce from local farms. We have written our summer menus in such a way that we can use the fleeting appearances of different vegetables and fruits as they come into season rather than tying the menu to specific produce and this is so exciting for us in the kitchen and hopefully also in the dining room.

Biting into fresh corn produces an explosion of toothsome buttery sweetness, and our August table d'hôte can't ever resist its siren call. The same is true for wild blueberries now in season from further up the road towards Abitibi and Baskatong Reservoir regions. The slack and bland year-round blueberry available from points south seems to bear little relationship in flavour and texture to the smaller, firm and sharp wild blueberry of the Canadian north.

As autumn approaches some leaves have begun to turn colour. "Nature's perfect design" – the acorn – hangs sculpted in the oaks, ready to fall.

Depending on the weather and food supply we will often have occasional visits to our garbage bins by black bears. We are reminded of our shared place in the grand scheme of things.

Basil and Parmigiano Reggiano Mousse

One 8" gâteau, 12 appetizer portions

This is the recipe we are most asked for year after year. It is like a savoury cheesecake with the strong flavours of fresh basil and Parmigiano Reggiano – perfect to serve on garden tomatoes still sun-warmed from the vine with some toasted pine nuts, lemon zest and good olive oil. This mousse also makes a delicious sandwich filling and has been a great crowd pleaser at buffets over the years.

1 cup fresh ricotta cheese
1 cup fresh cream cheese
1 cup sour cream
1 cup freshly grated
   Parmigiano Reggiano
4 whole eggs
2 cloves of garlic
juice of 2 lemons
1 tbsp flour
2 tbsp melted butter
grated nutmeg
salt and pepper
4 cups fresh basil leaves,
   cleaned and dried

In a food processor, process the cream cheese, ricotta, sour cream and Parmigiano until smooth. Add eggs, garlic, lemon juice, flour, butter and seasoning. Process again until smooth.

Add basil and process until smooth and emerald green. Pour mixture into a greased 8" springform pan. Bake at 275°F for 50 minutes. Allow to cool, then cover and refrigerate for at least 6 hours before unmoulding.

To serve, slice with a hot knife or shape into quenelles and serve on tomatoes drizzled with extra-virgin olive oil and sprinkled with pine nuts. Garnish with a parmesan tuile if desired.

Parmesan tuile
6 tuiles

1 cup grated Parmigiano
   Reggiano

Sprinkle grated Parmigiano Reggiano on parchment lined baking sheet in six 3" disks. Place in 300°F oven until golden. Remove from oven and lift tuiles off parchment with a thin metal spatula. Quickly roll into a cigarette shape while still warm and pliable. Use to garnish Basil and Parmigiano Reggiano Mousse, if desired.

Grilled Wild Nunavik Caribou served on Radicchio Chiffonade

with a Basil, Mint, Tarragon and Anchovy Salsa Verde

6 servings

Because of caribou's migratory habit, it is an animal that cannot be domesticated. As a result, this is one of the very few truly wild meats available to us. Improbably, this majestic King of the North feeds primarily on tiny lichens growing in the ground cover. Searching the taiga and tundra for these lichens is what impels its awesome migration. Caribou meat is as delicious as the very best steak plus it is higher in protein and iron than beef and lower in fat. We source most of our caribou through cooperatives operating out of northern Québec (Nunavik) where they hunt and process caribou from the George and Leaf River herds following rigorous ecological standards.

In summer we often offer grilled escalopes of caribou leg with salsa verde and slightly bitter radicchio tossed with Parmigiano Reggiano, aged balsamic vinegar and extra-virgin olive oil. The interplay of different but complementary textures, flavours and temperatures make this dish memorable. If caribou is not available, any other good quality red meat can be substituted (such as Black Angus beef from Priest Creek Farm).

12 escalopes of thinly
   sliced caribou leg
   ($2\frac{1}{2}$ ounces each)

Marinade

$\frac{1}{2}$ cup white wine

$\frac{1}{2}$ cup balsamic vinegar

1 tbsp crushed juniper
   berries

$\frac{1}{2}$ tbsp cracked black
   peppercorns

3 garlic cloves, sliced

$\frac{1}{2}$ cup vegetable oil

Whisk together marinade ingredients. Marinate escalopes for up to 2 hours. Drain well before grilling.

Grill escalopes on high heat very briefly – about 30 seconds per side.

Radicchio chiffonade

2 heads of radicchio
1 cup grated Parmigiano
  Reggiano
$\frac{3}{4}$ cup extra-virgin olive oil
$\frac{1}{2}$ cup balsamic vinegar
fresh thyme
salt and pepper

Cut radicchio into thin chiffonade or strips. Toss with remaining ingredients and adjust seasoning to taste.

Salsa verde

$\frac{1}{4}$ cup Dijon mustard
$\frac{1}{4}$ cup balsamic vinegar
$\frac{1}{4}$ cup capers
8 anchovy fillets
$\frac{1}{2}$ cup each basil, mint,
  Italian parsley, tarragon
  and coriander leaves
$\frac{1}{4}$ cup grated Parmigiano
  Reggiano
1 cup extra-virgin olive oil

Process all ingredients together in food processor until smooth.

Garnish

edible flower petals
Parmigiano Reggiano
lemon zest
cracked black pepper

To serve:

Place dressed chiffonade on centre of plate. Place caribou on chiffonade and top with a spoonful of salsa verde. Garnish with edible flower petals and curls of Parmigiano Reggiano, lemon zest and cracked black pepper. Serve with roasted new potatoes finished with white wine, garlic and rosemary, if desired.

Grilled Vegetables

A quick marinade in soy and olive oil and then onto the grill...

Slice zucchini, eggplant and seeded red and green peppers about $\frac{1}{2}$" thick. Toss vegetables in equal amount of extra-virgin olive oil and soy sauce to cover. Place on hot grill and cook on one side for 3-4 minutes. Remove to serving dish and sprinkle with fresh herbs, fleur de sel, extra-virgin olive oil and aged balsamic vinegar.

Summer Fruits in a Lemon Verbena and Mint Tea

accompanied by a Wild Blueberry Financier

4-6 servings

In this recipe, steeping Earl Grey tea with lemon verbena and mint from the garden with a little sugar produces a glorious, light syrup to complement summer fruits. This, to us, is a wonderful kind of summer dessert that does not interfere with the fruits, as they are already perfect. At most, we sometimes slip a spoonful of lemon sorbet into the bowl. A financier is an addictive little almond cake with a crisp exterior and slightly chewy inside. When currants or blueberries are in season we often sprinkle these over the batter as it goes into the oven.

$\frac{1}{2}$ cup sugar

4 cups water

1 lemon, juiced and zested

1 orange, juiced and zested

1 vanilla bean, split

$1\frac{1}{2}$ tbsp loose Earl Grey tea

6 fresh lemon verbena leaves, thinly sliced or 1 tsp minced fresh lemongrass

12 mint leaves, thinly sliced

selection of summer berries and stone fruits

Bring sugar and water to a boil over high heat.

Place remaining ingredients except fruit in a large bowl and pour hot syrup over. Let steep until cool then strain through a fine-mesh sieve. Cover with plastic wrap and refrigerate until cold.

Dice fruits. Leave small berries whole. Place $\frac{1}{2}$ cup of fruit in a shallow soup bowl and ladle 1 cup of tea over the berries. Garnish with sprig of mint or lemon verbena and serve with wild blueberry financier (recipe follows).

Wild Blueberry Financiers

3 dozen

1 cup butter
2½ cups icing sugar
½ cup flour
½ ground almonds
7 egg whites
sliced almonds for garnish
2 cups fresh wild
    blueberries

Brown butter: bring to a boil over high heat in a heavy-bottomed pot. The butter will foam up then subside, and the milk solids will begin to turn brown on the bottom of the pot. Swirl the pot occasionally and when the butter is a light caramel colour, remove from heat and immediately pour off liquid into a bowl. Discard browned bits. Let butter cool for 15 minutes.

Place icing sugar, flour and ground almonds in bowl of electric mixer with beater attachment. Mix on low speed until combined. Add egg whites and continue to mix on low speed until combined.

Scrape bottom and sides of bowl and continue to mix to remove lumps. You can mix on high for a few seconds if necessary, but do not incorporate too much air into mixture or cakes will be dry. Add cooled browned butter and mix on low speed until incorporated.

Pour into a parchment lined baking tray or mini-muffin trays, filling to the top. Sprinkle sliced almonds and wild blueberries on top, then bake at 400°F for about 30 minutes until cakes are puffed and golden brown, and spring back when pressed gently.

Let financiers rest until cool enough to handle, remove from baking tray or muffin moulds then finish cooling completely on racks. If using baking sheet, cut financier into slices.

Basil and Parmigiano Reggiano mousse on our own tomatoes

View from the dining room across the garden
and into the woodland

The clematis cresting the arbour

Neilon Donovan and Tammy McGarry of Priest
Creek Farm with their Black Angus

Photo courtesy PRIEST CREEK FARM

Grilled Nunavik caribou with salsa verde on radicchio chiffonade tossed with Parmigiano Reggiano, extra-virgin olive oil, aged balsamic and fresh thyme

Roast new potatoes with garlic, rosemary and white wine

Grilled August vegetables

Margot delivers gourmet products from Importations Tribeca and Itaca Direct: Portuguese sea salt, Amedei chocolate, SoTaroni moscatel vinegar, A l'Olivier and Galantino extra virgin olive oils and Bellei aged balsamic vinegar

Behind-the-scenes at a summer wedding in the Pavilion

Summer fruits in a lemon verbena and mint tea accompanied by wild blueberry financier

Wild blueberries from Abitibi, late harvest local strawberries and blackberries

September

The summer has streaked by non-stop. The crew at Les Fougères has been passing the baton between day and night shifts whilst running at full tilt through prep time, service and all that lies behind the scenes since mid-May. September stirs the pot in a few different directions – on the one hand business slows a little at the very beginning of the month, as many would-be guests are preoccupied with the transition to post-summer rhythms. On the other hand, these are some of the most beautiful days of the year: there is heat but it is not draining, the harvest is at its peak, the light has a new clearer quality to it and the idea of one last lingering lunch on the verandah is a temptation to which many succumb.

The first Monday in September is traditionally set aside for our annual staff party, held either at home by the Gatineau River or under our Summer Pavilion tent at Les Fougères. There have been many renditions and iterations of our staff party but it always involves lots of food, wine, music, dancing and a general end of summer meltdown between comrades and friends and their supportive families. At its very best a restaurant is a handmade project in a world of mass production. It is full of the possibilities and frailties of the team who make it up. The way in which we all try to allow strengths and gifts to shine while giving support in weaker areas is what lets the whole be something so much better than a simple sum of the parts. Life inside this country restaurant produces intensely close bonds amongst the staff, who depend on each other almost intimately. It is important to share some fun downtime together.

Purple aster, golden and rust helenium and an army of sunflowers of every type and height now dominate the garden. When we arrive in the mornings a cloud of chickadees and goldfinches rise out of the sunflowers, momentarily frightened from their feeding frenzy on the heavy seed heads of these magnificent flowers.

Almost as poignant as the first smell of freshly mown grass announcing the beginning of summer is the fragrance of tomato plants as you brush against them reaching for the perfect September tomato. This is the mouthwatering fragrance of late summer. The same is true of the prickle and scent that hit you when you wade through the sprawling squash plants. You feel as though you can smell and touch everything summer has worked for in this one moment.

The exhilarating variety and amount of produce pouring through our back door from farmer's fields and our own gardens is now almost overwhelming and one has two very different lines of thought: how to best make use of everything and, at the same time, fear in the knowledge that it will all be over too soon. In the store, we have a huge forty-gallon tilting skillet and a forty-gallon steam kettle – both are working at full throttle in September. This day they hold vegetables simmering in cider vinegar, sugar and spices as we take advantage of the harvest season for putting up our homemade pickles and chutneys. On other days the store will be scented with pestos, salsas, ketchups, fruit syrups, glazes, mustards and other condiments and sweet preserves as our canning reaches its peak.

The last of the season's wild mushrooms – ceps, lobster mushrooms and the occasional delight of a puffball – arrive at our back door and are the inspiration for heavenly specials on the menu. We are beginning to cut back and clean up the garden as well as plant in bulbs to bloom next spring.

As the month progresses we notice the weaker late afternoon light is likely to catch the tops of trees whose leaves have turned towards fall colours. Light is so amplified by the incipient golds of fall that it seems to be coming out of the trees themselves. The autumn equinox arrives and from here daylight will be shorter than night until spring again. Crisp, sharp, aromatic new crop apples overflow from farmer's market stands;

hummingbirds and butterflies have disappeared; birds on their way south have taken up a flocking habit, just as they did in springtime; and arrow after loose arrow of geese, hundreds strong, cut their way southward high in the sky. Clouds and swirling mists bank up on the Gatineau River after cold nights when the cooler air meets warmer water and one feels on the cusp of another quarter turn in the wheel of the seasons.

Many artists have set down roots in this area, drawn in part, no doubt, by the distinct beauty and power of our surroundings and changing seasons. Tours of local artists' workshops and hikes into the Gatineau Park often gild a late September trip into the Gatineau Hills taken to experience the spectacular show of vibrant colour that the woods now offer up. Many will drop into the store or restaurant on their way in or on their way back and we are thankful for this – yet another blessing of nature's beauty!

Beets and Tender Garden Greens

with Pistachios and Warm Rassembleu Vinaigrette served in a Gougère

6 servings

Gougères are the savoury version of pâte à choux – the dough used to make profiteroles, éclairs and cream puffs. The gorgeous little cheese puffs are a wonderful presentation for this beet salad. The warm dressing uses the beautiful raw milk artisanal blue cheese, Rassembleu, from the Laurentides, and has a classic affinity with sweet, just-pulled beets from the garden. If you cannot find Rassembleu, another blue cheese could be substituted.

Salad

4 cups tender mixed greens
6 beets, cooked, peeled
    and sliced
½ cup shelled pistachios,
    if desired

Gougères

1 cup water
3 tbsp butter
1 tsp salt
1 cup flour
4 eggs
freshly ground black pepper
2 ounces grated Gré des
    Champs from Montérégie,
    Québec, or Fribourg
    Gruyère
2 ounces grated
    Parmigiano Reggiano

Place water, butter and salt in a large pot. Bring to a boil then add flour all at once. Stir vigorously to remove lumps. Cook, stirring constantly, until dough pulls away from sides of pot in one large mass. Remove from heat and beat for one minute with wooden spoon to cool mixture slightly.

Place in food processor and, with motor running, add eggs one at a time. Add pepper and cheeses just until combined.

Place 2-ounce balls on baking sheet, spaced well apart. Bake at 400°F for 15-20 minutes until hollow when tapped. Allow to cool completely.

Dressing

$\frac{3}{4}$ cup Rassembleu
$\frac{1}{3}$ cup white wine
1 cup Classic
  vinaigrette (page 58)
2 tbsp chopped fresh
  rosemary

Place all ingredients in a small frying pan or pot. Warm gently over medium heat, whisking constantly until cheese melts and mixture emulsifies. Do not boil or dressing will split.

To assemble:

Split open gougère. Place salad greens, sliced beets and pistachios attractively in gougère. Pour some of the warm dressing onto greens and beets.

Caribou and Wild Boar Terrine with Cranberries and Hazelnuts

1 terrine of 12-15 portions

Some people are intimidated by the thought of making charcuterie. This rough-style country terrine is very easy and full of flavour. At Les Fougères, we serve Lady Ross mustard pickle and East India tomato relish with the terrine.

1 pound sliced bacon
6 ounces ground caribou
6 ounces ground wild boar
6 ounces ground veal
6 ounces ground pork
4 ounces diced lardons
1 tbsp juniper berries
1 tsp allspice berries
$\frac{1}{2}$ tsp whole cloves
2 unpeeled oranges,
  chopped, no seeds
6 ounces chicken livers
4 garlic cloves
1 tsp grated nutmeg
$\frac{1}{4}$ cup flour
2 tbsp butter, plus extra
  for sautéing
1 onion, diced
$\frac{1}{2}$ cup skinless hazelnuts
$\frac{3}{4}$ cup dried cranberries
1 tsp fresh thyme
1 bay leaf, crushed
$\frac{1}{2}$ cup brandy
$\frac{1}{4}$ cup whipping cream
salt and pepper to taste

Line terrine mould (12 $''$ x 2$\frac{1}{2}$ $''$ x 3 $''$) with sliced bacon (be sure to leave some for the top).

Combine ground meats and diced bacon in a large stainless steel mixing bowl. Grind together juniper berries, allspice and cloves and set aside.

Process chopped orange, chicken livers and garlic in food processor to a rough chop. Add nutmeg and ground spices and process again until well mixed. Add processed mixture to ground meats with flour and butter.

Sauté diced onion in extra butter with hazelnuts, cranberries, thyme and bay leaf until golden brown. Add brandy and flambé. Add cream. Cool. Add onion mixture to ground meat mixture and adjust seasoning to taste.

Pack mixture into prepared mould. Cover top with more bacon slices, then cover with lid. Place terrine mould in a roasting pan and pour boiling water halfway up the sides of the terrine. Bake in a 375°F oven for $1\frac{3}{4}$ hours. Make sure terrine is cooked by inserting a skewer into the middle and checking that the juices which flow out of the skewer hole are clear. Remove from roasting pan, weight down lightly and let cool completely.

To serve:

Slice with a sharp knife and serve with Lady Ross and East India pickles (recipes follow).

Lady Ross Mustard Pickle

Approximately ten 8-ounce jars

We often wonder who Lady Ross was and whether she indeed was actually the one to get down and chop the vegetables… This is a much treasured old family recipe and now also the top-selling homemade condiment in our store

1 cup peeled, seeded and
   chopped cucumber
1 cup peeled and chopped
   onion
1 cup peeled pearl onions
4 cups water
½ cup salt
1 cup chopped pickled
   gherkins
1 cup chopped celery
1 cup chopped red pepper
3 cups sugar
¼ cup mustard seed
3 cups cider vinegar

½ cup mustard powder
¼ cup flour
½ tbsp turmeric
½ cup cider vinegar

Cover cucumber, onion and pearl onions with water and salt. Stir and leave overnight. Drain and rinse well.

In a stockpot, combine rinsed onion and cucumber mixture, celery, gherkins, red pepper, sugar, mustard seed and 1 cup cider vinegar. Bring to a boil and boil for 10 minutes. Meanwhile, make up the mustard paste by processing until smooth the mustard powder, flour, turmeric and remaining cider vinegar in a food processor. Add little by little to boiling vegetable mixture, stirring all the time to avoid lumps.

Boil for another 5-10 minutes until onions and cucumbers are clear. Pour into hot sterilized jars and seal.

East India Tomato Relish

Approximately ten 8-ounce jars

Like the Lady Ross pickle, another favourite family recipe.

20 ripe tomatoes
4 large cooking onions,
    chopped
4 large red peppers,
    chopped
2 large green peppers,
    chopped
4 tbsp salt
4 cups cider vinegar
4 cups granulated sugar

To peel tomatoes:
Bring a large pot of water to a boil. Prepare a bowl of ice water. Cut an X across the bottom of each tomato. Place the tomatoes in boiling water for 15-20 seconds, then remove using a slotted spoon and plunge immediately into the ice water to stop cooking. Remove from ice water and peel away the skin.

Chop tomatoes coarsely.

Combine tomatoes, onion, peppers and salt in a large pot. Bring to a simmer over medium heat. Reduce heat to low and continue to cook for $\frac{1}{2}$ hour, stirring occasionally.

Add the vinegar and the sugar and stir to combine. Continue to cook over low heat for 2 more hours, stirring so that bottom does not burn, until relish is desired thickness.

Pour into sterilized jars and seal.

Cortland Apple Tartlet

8 servings

This recipe suggests making an unsweetened apple compote which is strained overnight, mounded on pastry disks and finished with a circle of thinly sliced apple and sugar. We love this technique because the result is a very pure, tart, new crop apple flavour in a presentation that does not weep – so it is lovely to look at and maintains its counterpoints between softened apple and sweet flaky pastry. A fragile sugar cage adds the wonderful flavour and texture of caramel as well as some bling-bling! Cortland, Macintosh or Lobo are our favourite new crop apples. In the middle of winter, however, it is the Macintosh which still retains good sharpness.

Apple compôte

16 Cortland apples
1 cup water

2 cups sugar for
    shaking on top of
    compôte

Peel, core and chop 12 apples (remaining 4 will be used to top tartlets). Cook down slowly with water in a large saucepan. When apples are soft, place in a sieve and drain overnight into a container. Sweeten the drained juice to taste and reserve. Remove the strained apple compote from the sieve and reserve.

Pastry

2 cups flour
pinch of salt
1 cup cold butter, in
    cubes
$\frac{3}{4}$ cup cold water

Pulse the flour and salt with the butter cubes in a food processor until mixture has the texture of breadcrumbs. With the processor running, add cold water gradually, just until the dough forms a ball. Wrap in plastic and chill in fridge.

To assemble tartlets:

Roll out pastry to $\frac{1}{4}$" thick. Cut out 4" rounds and chill.

Place 8 rounds on a baking sheet well spaced out. Using a 2-ounce ice cream scoop, place a scoop of the strained apple compote in the centre of each round.

Place very thin apple slices from 2 cored but not peeled apples in a neat circle on top of compote. Shake a generous coating of sugar onto tartlets.

Bake at 375°F for 15 minutes or until the pastry is golden and flaky, and the apple mixture is bubbling.

Serve with the reserved apple juice, a caramel cage or twist (see page 90) and crème fraîche or maple syrup ice cream.

Caramel Cages and Twists

2 cups sugar

$\frac{1}{4}$ cup water

1-2 drops of fresh lemon juice

Swirl together the sugar, water and lemon juice in a pan over high heat until the sugar is dissolved. Simmer until the syrup has become a light amber caramel. Let the mixture cool until it is the consistency of molasses. Grease the outside of a large soup ladle. Stir the caramel with a fork and lift the fork so that the caramel collected on the fork runs from it in a thick thread. Hold the ladle in one hand with the outside of the bowl facing upward and make a grid work of caramel on the upturned ladle by moving your caramel-loaded fork back and forth. Be sure to wrap a few extra lines of caramel around the bottom edge to reinforce the "cage". The caramel will cool in seconds and you will be able to lift the cage from the ladle.

For caramel twists, let the caramel cool even more than for cage making so that when you lift the fork out of the caramel you are pulling out a caramel thread (which has been cooled beyond the running-off-the-fork stage). Rotate your fork around a plastic tube (a sausage making tube works well) pulling the thread of caramel into a twist along the length of tube as you go. The caramel cools in seconds and you can slip the caramel twist off the tube. (*see photographs following September and November*)

Gougère with our beets and salad greens
and a warm Rassembleu dressing

Sunflowers dominate
the gardens in September

Caribou and wild boar terrine with cranberries and hazelnuts, served with Lady Ross mustard pickle and East India tomato relish

Jean-Luc raises wild boar at La Ferme Par Toutatis

Merci
Thank-you

Les Fougères Annual Staff Party

Previous page: Cortland apple tartlet with maple ice cream and a caramel cage

October

October is the month in which Canadian Thanksgiving falls. There is always much to be thankful for.

Local ski hills start up their chairlifts at this time of year so we can travel, awestruck, to the top of our corner of the mighty Canadian Shield. From there one sees an undulating carpet of dazzling autumn colour stretching out northeastward towards the distant Laurentians. The hills and valleys of this region are covered in mixed forest dominated by deciduous hardwoods, each adding their unique hue to the mix – the reds and oranges of the maple, the yellows of the birch, the orange-browns of the oak, the yellow-browns of the beech, the reddish-green of the ash. To all this is added the velvety red berry spikes of the sumac, the surprising bright yellow needles of the tamarack and the scarlet of Virginia creepers. No wonder visitors and locals alike pack the roads and trails at this time of year! We are so happy to welcome some of them with a new menu which has moved from summer fare towards more use of the condiments, preserves and accents we have put up and stocked in the larder from summer's bounty. In addition, we turn to the intense, concentrated flavours of dried wild mushrooms; delicious root stock vegetables which are now coming into their own; the fleeting potency of new crop apples, and the slow-cooked braises and casseroles which open up the deep tenor flavour notes in meats such as hare, deer, wild boar, lamb and beef, most of which are supplied to us by nearby farmers.

Early October is the time to finish picking the crabapples and to make the pectin-rich crabapple stock we use as a base for most of our homemade jellies – crabapple and rosemary being one of our favourites.

Now is also the time for our peculiar ritual of "hydrangea scrunching." The Peegee hydrangea, especially, has beautiful distended plumes of delicate petals that take on a blush of pink as the colder season progresses. If you can cut branches from the bush when the weather has turned colder and the plumes of blossom are beginning to feel slightly 'papery' but have not yet succumbed to an overnight frost, then you can let these branches dry inside where the colour will not fade and the graceful dignity of the blooms will not wilt. The view held by many that dried flower arrangements are dusty and overstuffed is banished by the sight of a few stalks of rosy hued hydrangea standing sparely in a vase, catching the light on the windowsill, or by the massed arrangement of hydrangea on our granite hewn fireplace mantle. We also try to catch just the right moment to cut beech leaf branches and set them in glycerin water to preserve the bronze sunshine in their leaves, and to cut ornamental grasses, such as miscanthus sinensis, bullrushes and Chinese lanterns to preserve them before they, too, give in to a frost.

The techniques of preserving and arranging are arts that have been honed by Joan Warren over a lifetime in step with plants and flowers. She understands their ways and particular characteristics. Over the last 14 years Joan has visited the restaurant twice a week, rarely so much as accepting a cup of tea, to pick and bring flowers and to create arrangements in our window bays which celebrate each stalk and bloom. She generously teaches us about her beloved plant world and we are an appreciative audience.

A nice sunny day in mid October is also a good time to try to "pot up" – that is, to plant some spring bulbs (which we held back from planting into the ground last month) into pots which we will then keep at just above freezing until about mid-February whilst they develop their thread-like root work. We will then place them in a less cold, but still very cool place until shoots gloriously begin to emerge out of the soil. Once the shoots have lengthened and developed bud we will crowd the pots inside along our window bays and sills in the restaurant and enjoy them coming into spring bloom. This is even before the snow outside has disappeared due to our mimicking of winter and spring that has "forced" the plants to bloom early. The easiest bulbs to force are daffodils. The pleasure they give and the gratifying link back to this crisp and bright day in October is enormously special. Hallowe'en comes at the end of the month and we circle the verandah with candle-lit pumpkins with carved out faces on two sides: one pointing to the outside so people driving by can see and one pointing in towards the windows of the restaurant to be seen by our guests – even if they are trying to avoid trick-or-treaters at home by hiding at the restaurant! Every year the bar is raised as the standard of carving becomes more and more accomplished. The sight of the restaurant as night falls with a big basket of treats at the front door and the pumpkins all around with their wavering orange light against the blue black sky is one for the memory bank and another marker in the wheel of time as the year moves along.

By the end of the month, autumn's blazing colour has gone as the leaves have quietly dropped or been torn away in whipping October winds. What might have been dew at the beginning of the month is now morning hoar frost or even a veil of snow. Most migrating birds have long since caught the Atlantic flyway southward. Many fir trees have become sticky and tacky as they fill up with resin that will act like anti-freeze in the coming frigid months. The chipmunks should have their storehouses of acorns ready for the winter hibernation. For our part it has been a busy summer and fall and the gears shift a bit towards taking stock as well as thinking ahead to preparations for Christmas…

Terrine of Foie Gras with Duck Confit, Armagnac and Prunes

1 terrine

This is made by layering duck confit and prunes between thick slices of pure foie gras terrine. A few drops of delicious duck fat keep the confit and prunes firm enough to produce a clean slice where the layers do not slip away from each other. Since Armagnac, prunes and duck (both as meat and foie gras) are all very complementary to each other, this terrine produces a luscious and luxurious foie gras experience.

1 cup pitted prunes, sliced in half

½ cup Armagnac (1st amount)

2 lobes fresh foie gras

1 tbsp sea salt

½ cup Armagnac (2nd amount)

3 legs of duck confit

Soak prunes in Armagnac for at least ½ hour.

Clean lobes by separating foie from any veins and sinews gently with your hands. Smooth deveined foie gras in a thin, even layer on a baking tray. Sprinkle with salt and Armagnac. Cover with plastic wrap and place in fridge overnight.

Press foie gras into a 12″ x 2½″ x 3″ terrine mould. Place in a bain marie and bake at 275°F for 20 minutes. Place a weight on the terrine and refrigerate overnight.

Warm the duck leg confit to make it easier to remove the meat. Remove meat from legs of duck confit and combine with drained, Armagnac-infused prunes, along with a few tablespoons of the duck fat which will have come out of the warmed confit legs.

Remove the chilled, cooked foie gras from the terrine mould and slice it. Into a clean 12″ x 2½″ x 3″ terrine mould lined with plastic wrap, layer the confit and prune mixture alternating with the foie gras. Begin and end with the confit and prunes to give three layers of confit and prunes and two layers of foie gras. Cover with plastic wrap. Press down well and refrigerate overnight.

Crabapple and Rosemary Jelly

Approximately six 6-ounce jars

Crabapples have a lot of natural pectin. At this time of year we use our own crabapples as well as cases bought in to make crabapple pectin stock that we store in the freezer. To make pectin stock: Quarter stemmed crabapples. Barely cover with water and simmer until pulpy. Place in a jelly bag over a large bowl overnight. Do not press. Place strained juice in a pot and reduce by half. Ladle into measured containers and freeze for future use. One half cup of this pectin stock should set at least 2 cups of fruit or pure fruit juice. It is great to have it on hand to help set jams and jellies from less pectin-rich fruit such as blackberries and strawberries. We also use this beautiful, flavourful, rosy crabapple juice to enrich sauces (especially for pork and wild boar) and also as a base for sorbets (both as dessert and as a palate-cleanser). Crabapple-rosemary jelly is superb served with ham, pork, chicken and cheese.

4 pounds crabapples, stems removed

water to cover

1 cup apple cider vinegar

2 tbsp chopped fresh rosemary (1st amount)

sugar as required (see method)

2 tbsp chopped fresh rosemary (2nd amount)

Cut stemmed crabapples into quarters. Put into a pot with barely enough water to cover and add apple cider vinegar and first amount of rosemary. Cook until fruit is mushy. Pour into a jelly bag with a pan underneath and leave overnight. Don't press – just allow the fruit to gently release its clear juice. The next day, measure the amount of juice you have into a large pot. For every $2\frac{1}{2}$ cups of crabapple juice add 2 cups of sugar. Dissolve the sugar over medium-low heat, then increase heat to high and boil rapidly until the setting point is reached (a small amount of the jelly is spooned onto a saucer and placed into the fridge to cool for 5 minutes. If, after these 5 minutes, the saucer is tilted and the jelly wrinkles, then it is ready.) Stir in second amount of rosemary. Pour into hot, sterilized jars and seal.

Seared Grand Banks Scallops served on Fundy Smoked Haddock Risotto

with Matane Shrimps, Coriander, Pear and Curry Spices

6 servings

The origin of this recipe is a dish called "kedgeree" which Charlie (and many children in England) were brought up on. Kedgeree is a rice dish with kippers, curry spices, peas and hard-boiled eggs which itself has its roots in the days of the British Raj in India. Charlie always loved the intersecting smoky, sweet and spicy elements of kedgeree and has often returned to these haunting flavours in his own menus. In this kedgeree-inspired risotto dish we use the wonderful flavour of smoked haddock. The smokiness of the haddock is partnered with a little sweetness from pear, scallop, peas and Matane shrimp and the exotic complexity of freshly roasted and ground spices.

Homemade curry powder

1 tbsp cumin seeds

1 tbsp cardamom

1 tbsp coriander seeds

3 whole star anise

1″ piece cinnamon stick

$\frac{1}{4}$ tbsp black peppercorns

$\frac{1}{4}$ tbsp cloves

$\frac{1}{4}$ tbsp fennel seed

Roast all ingredients together in a dry frying pan over medium heat briefly (1-2 minutes), shaking pan constantly, until fragrant and beginning to toast. Grind to a fine powder.

For the risotto

2 boneless fillets smoked
   haddock
1 cup whipping cream
½ cup butter
1 onion, diced
2 celery stalks, chopped
1 tbsp chopped fresh
   ginger
1 tbsp chopped garlic
1 tbsp fresh homemade
   curry powder – see above
2 cups Carnaroli rice
3 cups hot chicken stock
1 cup white wine
1 cup pear juice
4 poached pears, chopped
1 cup Matane shrimps
½ cup mascarpone cheese
1 cup frozen peas
1 tbsp fresh chopped
   coriander
zest of 1 orange
salt and pepper to taste

For the seared scallops

½ cup butter
24 sea scallops (16/20)*
fleur de sel and freshly
   cracked black pepper
   to season

Cover the haddock filets with the cream and bring to a boil. Reduce heat to low and poach very gently until the haddock is cooked and tender and flakes easily. Reserve.

Meanwhile, gently sweat onion and celery in butter until softened. Add the ginger, garlic and curry powder. Add the rice and let it "toast" for a couple of minutes. Warm the stock, wine and pear juice and add, little by little, to the rice, stirring constantly and making sure the rice absorbs all the liquid before adding more. This will take about 16 minutes. After the last addition of liquid add the flaked smoked haddock and cream as well as chopped pears, shrimps, mascarpone, peas, coriander and orange zest. Heat through and check for seasoning.

For the scallops, melt the butter in two wide sauté pans over high heat. Place the scallops in the pans in a single layer. Do not crowd and do not move the scallops until you see that they are nicely golden on the pan side. Give the pans a shake to turn the scallops over then remove the pans from the heat and let the scallops sit for several minutes. Season.

(*Scallops and shrimp are sized by "count". In this case, a 16/20 count means that 16-20 scallops would make up a pound, ie: each scallop is 1 oz or slightly smaller.)

To serve:

Spoon the risotto onto 6 plates or shallow soup bowls. Place 4 seared scallops on top of risotto on each plate. Garnish with orange zest and fresh coriander.

Hazelnut Dacquoise
layered with Prune and Armagnac Sorbet

1 dacquoise, 8-10 servings

Another delicious use for one of our favourite combinations – prunes and Armagnac.

Hazelnut dacquoise

$1\frac{1}{4}$ cups egg whites
$1\frac{1}{2}$ cups sugar
1 ounce Frangelico liqueur
$1\frac{1}{2}$ cups ground hazelnuts
$1\frac{1}{2}$ tbsp cornstarch

Whip whites with $\frac{3}{4}$ cup sugar to soft peaks. Add Frangelico and continue to whip to stiff peaks.

Combine nuts, cornstarch and remaining sugar. Fold into whites in 3 additions. Spread evenly onto a Silpat or parchment-lined 12″ x 16″ baking sheet.

Bake at 350°F until golden and centre is no longer wet, about 40 minutes. Rotate pan halfway through baking.

Cool the pan until easy to handle. Run a knife along the edges of the biscuit then flip over and carefully pry out of pan, using the Silpat if necessary. Peel off Silpat.

Using a serrated knife, slice off uneven and/or brittle edges. Slice lengthwise into 3 equal strips.

Prune and armagnac sorbet

2 packages of pitted prunes (750 g each)
1 cup Armagnac
2-3 cups orange juice
1 cup sugar

Combine all ingredients in a large pot. Gently bring to a boil, stirring occasionally to dissolve sugar and to be sure prunes do not stick to bottom. Simmer over low heat, partially covered, until liquid is mostly absorbed and prunes have started to break down. You may need to add a little more orange juice during cooking if all the liquid is absorbed.

Remove from heat and blend to a smooth purée in blender or food processor. Freeze in ice cream maker according to manufacturer's directions. Scoop into a clean container, cover tightly and freeze for 2-3 hours to firm up.

To assemble dacquoise:

Remove sorbet from freezer. If sorbet is very hard, let stand for a few minutes at room temperature to soften slightly. Place 1 slice of dacquoise on counter. Carefully spread sorbet over biscuit to about $\frac{3}{4}$" thick. Repeat with second dacquoise slice (it's easier to do them both directly on the counter first) then stack one on top of the other. Top with third dacquoise slice. Press down lightly to ensure sorbet fills all layers evenly.

Use a spatula to even out sides of dacquoise, adding sorbet or trimming it away to the edge of the biscuit where needed. Wrap tightly in plastic wrap and return to freezer for 3-4 hours to firm up completely.

To serve, remove from freezer and slice with large, sharp knife into 1-1$\frac{1}{2}$" wide portions. Serve with raspberry sauce and a caramel twist (see recipe on page 90 and photograph opposite page 111).

Raspberry sauce:

3 cups raspberries
sugar to taste

Gently simmer raspberries and sugar together for 10 minutes. Pass through a fine sieve to remove seeds. Cool and serve.

Drying and Preserving

During the growing season we generally have lots of fresh flower arrangements, using flowers picked from our own gardens. In fall and winter we can still have distinctive and stunning natural arrangements using some of the following preserving techniques.

Dried hydrangeas

Cut long branches off PeeGee hydrangea bushes in October when the blossoms feel slightly papery or crispy but before there has been a frost. Place these stems carefully upright in a place where they will not get crushed against each other. A good solution is to cut the stems long and set them in an empty cardboard wine box with its original dividers. Let the hydrangea dry for several weeks. They will keep their lovely colour and shape.

Preserved beech leaves

Cut nice long branches of beech in September and October just before the leaves begin to change colour. Make up a mixture of two parts glycerin (available at the pharmacy) to one part water. Lightly crush the stem ends of the branches with a hammer and place these in the glycerin solution. Do not disturb for several weeks until the leaves have become papery and golden-brown. The branches and leaves are now preserved and can be used in arrangements.

Dried ornamental grass and bullrushes

Miscanthus sinensis is an ornamental grass that produces attractive feathery plumes on tall stalks in October. If they are cut and brought inside after they have produced their feathery plume, the plume will shed like a spent dandelion. If, however, they are cut just before their feathery plume opens, they can be brought inside to create stunning arrangements because the plume will open up but will not shed. Likewise, bullrushes should be cut for drying well before they explode with fluff. Indeed, September is a good month to cut bullrushes and to bring them inside to dry.

Making Bay of Fundy smoked haddock risotto

Seared Grand Banks scallops on smoked
haddock risotto with coriander, pear and freshly roasted
and ground curry spices

Picking and drying Peegee hydrangeas; arrangement of dried hydrangeas over the fireplace in the dining room

Beech leaves along the woodland trail ready for cutting and preserving in glycerin

Arrangement of dried beech leaves, ferns and bullrushes

Picking miscanthus sinensis at just the right moment

Finished arrangement of *miscanthus sinensis* in the dining room

Crabapple trees through to the end of October

Deveining Québec foie gras for terrine layered with duck confit and Armagnac prunes; Ian Walker of Mariposa Farms stops by with a feathered friend; jack-o-lanterns glow on Hallowe'en night

CTP/JMP

November

The glory days of fall are over and the exhilaration of fresh new snow which lasts is yet to come. The days are quickly shortening and becoming colder. Six or seven cords of dry hardwood are delivered and stacked on our balcony and daily fires in our granite fireplace begin.

November is one of the quietest months in terms of guests to the restaurant but the slower pace in the dining room is in total contrast to the buzz of activity underway to prepare the store for Christmas. Thousands of tourtières are being made; dried fruit, citrus peel and suet are steeped in rum in preparation for traditional Christmas puddings and cakes; and we are building a stockroom of Christmas cookies, biscotti, Bûches de Noël, truffles, caramels, real fruit jellies, financiers, sugared and spiced nuts, preserved lemons and sweet pickled ginger. We are also doubling up on our regular line of soups, casseroles, pâtés, terrines, sausages, curries, vinaigrettes, confit and canapés.

Upstairs, above the restaurant, office space is transformed into a veritable Santa's workshop. Daily we receive carefully selected gourmet products that we hope will make special gifts to offer in the store. There are miles of ribbon and twine and stacks of baskets and tissue. The indomitable Paulette, who has been with us since we opened in 1993, will devote herself almost full-time now to putting together fabulous gift baskets. In short, November is December's workhorse for us here at Les Fougères and the apparent quiet in the dining room disguises a very exciting and busy time behind the scenes.

Outside, November usually strings together many cold, wet and monotone days under pewter skies. The trees are bare of leaves and the gardens have all been tidied and put to bed. The look is stark and ordered and ready for snow. The land is in a state of anticipation – just as we are inside.

One of our crabapple trees is still full of the tiny crabapples we do not pick because of their small size. This particular tree and its fruit will often attract itinerant visitors – on one day it is flush with more than a dozen beautiful Bohemian waxwings. On another day, during a Sunday brunch, everyone in the restaurant is treated to the sight of a usually stealthy and nocturnal fisher as he lopes out of the forest, climbs up the trunk and, beady-eyed, grabs at a few crabapples. Later, on a clear moonless night, we are stunned by a waving arc of northern light – pulsing green, yellow and purple – curling and spilling over itself back and forth from horizon to horizon. We are never without a sense of awe and gratitude to be here, part of all this, inside and out.

Homemade Lime Pickle

Roast, then grind together:

1″ stick of cinnamon

3 whole star anise

1 tsp whole coriander seed

1 tsp whole green cardamom seed

1 tsp whole cumin seed

4 whole cloves

6 limes

2 onions, sliced

1 tbsp vegetable oil

2 cloves garlic, crushed

2 tbsp grated fresh ginger

$\frac{1}{2}$ cup tomato paste

1 tbsp mustard seed

1 cup cider vinegar

1 cup sugar

2 tsp fenugreek leaves

1 tbsp chopped fresh coriander

salt and black pepper to taste

Place limes in a large pot and cover with cold water. Bring to a boil, reduce heat and simmer 40 minutes. Strain and, when limes are cool enough to handle, slice into quarters and spoon out interior. Try to reserve as much of the fruit as possible but discard the filaments and seeds. Chop peel and pulp coarsely in food processor and reserve.

In a heavy-bottomed pot over medium heat, sweat onions in oil until soft and translucent. Add chopped limes, garlic, ginger, freshly roasted and ground spices, tomato paste, mustard seed, cider vinegar and sugar. Reduce heat to low and simmer 45 minutes. Stir in fenugreek and coriander and season to taste.

Smoked Mackerel with Maple-Soy Glaze
served on a Timbale of Avocado, Red Onion and Potato Brunoise

6 servings

Atlantic mackerel has a lovely rich and unique flavour. It is a relatively oily fish, being high in healthy omega 3 and 6 fatty acids. We source our smoked mackerel from Willy Krauch in Nova Scotia where it is lightly peppered and hot smoked so it has a nice spiciness and light smokiness. We heighten this with a brushing of maple-soy glaze (salty and sweet) and a sprinkling of toasted sesame seeds after the fish is broiled. The avocado and potato timbale offers a luscious foil for the assertive complexity of the fish. Try it also using Willy Krauch smoked eel or with grilled wild arctic char. The maple-soy glaze is great to have on hand when you barbecue: just brush onto any grilled fish for a delicious twist.

2 avocados, peeled and
  chopped into small dice
2 Yukon Gold potatoes,
  peeled diced and cooked
2 tbsp finely chopped
  red onion
2 tbsp chopped
  coriander
¼ cup extra-virgin olive oil
salt and pepper to taste

6 pieces of smoked
  mackerel (2 ounces each)
½ cup maple-soy glaze
¼ cup toasted sesame
  seeds
orange zest

Place avocado and potato dice into a bowl. Add red onion, coriander and olive oil and toss gently until vegetables are nicely coated with a fine layer of oil. Season to taste with salt and pepper.

Place mackerel on a lightly greased baking sheet and broil. Brush generously with maple-soy glaze and return to broiler for 1 minutes until glaze bubbles. Sprinkle with toasted sesame seeds and fresh orange zest.

Gently pack ½ cup of avocado mixture into a lightly oiled ramekin, then turn over onto plate and unmould carefully. Place warm mackerel on potato-avocado timbale and drizzle a little extra maple-soy glaze around the plate for garnish.

Maple-soy glaze

Combine $\frac{1}{2}$ cup pure maple syrup and $\frac{1}{2}$ cup soy sauce in a small, heavy-bottomed pot. Bring to a boil, then reduce heat to medium and boil gently until reduced by half. Let cool completely. Can be stored in a sealed jar at room temperature for up to 1 month. If refrigerated, allow to warm up slightly to make it easier to pour.

Toasted sesame seeds

Place sesame seeds in a small frying pan over medium-high heat. Shake the pan constantly to stir the seeds as they begin to colour. When the seeds are fragrant, golden and some are starting to pop, remove from heat and immediately pour into a cool bowl (if you leave them in the pan, the residual heat in the pan may cause the seeds to burn).

Lamb and Apple Curry

8 servings

Curry was very much part of Charlie's culinary upbringing in the U.K. where family business ties to India as well as weekly meals at the local "Indian" were important and formative. Charlie has always been intrigued by the layering of flavours in Indian cuisine and has tried to apply traditional Indian techniques to achieve distinctive and authentic curries from scratch.

This lamb and apple curry is very popular at Les Fougères in the store and in the restaurant when it is on the menu. At this time of the year it is a wonderful way to use fresh local lamb and fall's new crop apples. Lamb shoulder with its delicious marbling is the best cut to use for this long, gentle braising where the lamb and freshly roasted and ground spices will deliciously intermingle. This is not really a hot curry – there is more fragrant spicing than heat with flavours such as cardamom, cloves, cinnamon, mint, apple and coconut.

Roast and grind together:

2 tsp whole cumin seed

2 tsp fennel seed

4 tsp whole coriander seed

2 tsp whole black peppercorns

2 whole star anise

2 tsp whole green cardamom pods

1 tsp whole cloves

1 lamb shoulder, cut into $\frac{3}{4}$" dice (about $2\frac{1}{2}$ pounds)

$\frac{1}{2}$ cup butter

1 cup olive oil

2 onions, chopped

2 green peppers, chopped

Place butter and olive oil in a large oven-proof pot on high heat. When fat is hot and almost smoking, add lamb and brown well on all sides. Add onions, green peppers, apples, garlic, ginger, chili peppers, shredded coconut and freshly roasted and ground spices and stir to combine.

Sprinkle turmeric over contents of pot. Add apple juice, coconut milk, cinnamon stick, tamarind paste and lime pickle. Add water to cover if necessary.

Place lid on pot and bake in a 375°F for 2 hours or until lamb is tender.

6 tart apples, chopped (such
    as Granny Smith)
4 ounces unsweetened
    shredded coconut
2 ounces garlic, chopped
2 ounces peeled fresh
    ginger, chopped
1-2 hot chili peppers,
    according to taste
1 tsp ground turmeric
1 litre fresh apple juice
1 litre coconut milk
1 cinnamon stick, about
    2″ long
1 tbsp tamarind paste
$\frac{1}{2}$ cup lime pickle (see
    recipe on page 103 or use
    a good quality prepared
    lime pickle)
2 tbsp fresh coriander
    leaves
1 cup fresh mint leaves,
    lightly packed

Remove from oven, skim away any fat that has come to the surface and finish with freshly chopped coriander and mint.

Garnish with sliced fresh banana and toasted coconut. Serve with basmati rice, minted yogurt, lime pickle and poppadum, a crisp chickpea or lentil flatbread available from Indian stores.

These are just a few of the favourite recipes we are making constantly at this time of year to keep our shelves stocked with goodies as the festive season approaches. Any of these would make great homemade Christmas presents.

Devilish Almonds

Six 8-ounce jars

2 pounds skinless almonds
4 tbsp Worcestershire sauce
2 tbsp soy sauce
6 cloves garlic
2 tsp salt, more if desired
1 tsp cayenne pepper,
　more if desired
1 tsp cumin
½ tsp ground black pepper
few dashes Tabasco
2 egg whites

Combine Worcestershire sauce through to Tabasco in food processor until garlic is completely puréed. Add egg whites and pulse just to blend.

Pour mixture over nuts in bowl and let stand 30 minutes, stirring occasionally.

Drain and reserve liquid. Spread on parchment-lined baking sheets and bake at 300°F about 10 minutes, until slightly dry. Baste with reserved liquid, adding salt if desired. Continue to bake, stirring occasionally, until dry and roasted, about 15-20 minutes.

Cool completely and store airtight at room temperature.

Butter Roasted Almonds with Cranberries and Sea Salt

Toss 1 pound skinless almonds with ½ cup melted butter to coat and sea salt to taste. Spread out on a parchment-lined baking sheet and roast at 325°F until golden brown, about 12 minutes, stirring occasionally. Cool completely, then mix with dried cranberries and a little more sea salt to taste. Store in an airtight container at room temperature.

Maple Balsamic Pecans

Toss 1 pound pecans with ¼ cup maple syrup and about ¼ cup of good balsamic vinegar to taste (look for a nice sweet/tangy balance). Roast on a parchment-lined baking sheet at 325°F until fragrant and glazed (approximately 15 minutes), then sprinkle generously with sea salt and let cool. Store in an airtight container at room temperature.

Honey Dijon Cashews

Combine 2 parts smooth Dijon to 1 part honey, some salt and a little melted butter to thin. The consistency should be loose and there should be a generous amount. Toss cashews with the honey mustard mixture. Don't let them sit or they'll get soggy. Spread out on a parchment-lined baking sheet and roast at 325°F, stirring every 5 minutes. Watch them carefully as they brown quickly! Remove from oven when golden. The nuts will still seem soggy but will crisp as they cool. Don't disturb until cool and dry. Store in an airtight container at room temperature.

Fleur de Sel Caramels

One 18" x 13" tray

4 cups sugar

1 cup water

3 cups glucose or white corn syrup

1 tsp salt

2 sticks butter, cut into pieces

4 cups cream

2 cups sweetened condensed milk

1 tbsp vanilla extract

$\frac{1}{4}$ cup fleur de sel, for sprinkling

Combine sugar, water, glucose or corn syrup and salt in a heavy-bottomed pot. Stir to combine then bring to a boil over high heat, washing down the sides of the pot with a wet pastry brush. Place a candy thermometer in the mixture and let it cook without stirring until the thermometer reads 250°F. Wash down the sides the pot again.

Add butter, stirring gently to help it melt. Gradually stir in 2 cups of cream. Bring to a boil and let it cook to reduce to almost half. During this time, the mixture will begin caramelizing and changing to its distinct colour. Stir in the remaining cream. Continue to boil, stirring in a figure eight motion, until the temperature reaches 250°F again. Remove from heat.

Stir in the condensed milk. Return to heat, stirring constantly, until the mixture reaches 244°F. Remove from heat and continue to stir for 2 minutes; it will start to thicken. Stir in the vanilla. Pour into Silpat or parchment-lined pan. When cooler but still tacky, sprinkle with fleur de sel. Leave uncovered at room temperature overnight. Unmould and cut into squares with a cold knife.

Preserved Lemons

2 jars large enough to hold 2 lemons each

Preserved lemons are delicious sliced and added to slow-cooked braises and casseroles, especially lamb.

4 lemons
⅓ cup sea salt
⅓ cup sugar
3″ cinnamon stick
1 teaspoon black peppercorns
2 teaspoons coriander seed
6 cloves
3 whole star anise

Add lemons to 4 cups of boiling water and continue to boil for 5 minutes. Remove lemons, reserving the water, and when they are cool enough to handle slice in quarters, keeping them attached at the stem end. Pack lemons into sterilized jars. Add salt, sugar and the spices to the reserved water and bring to a boil for 10 minutes. Cover the lemons with the boiling spiced water syrup. Seal jars and refrigerate. Let sit for at least 3 weeks before using.

Pickled Ginger

Approximately six 8-ounce jars

It is particularily nice to make your own pickled ginger because commercial varieties so often include artificial colouring and sweetening agents. We often use sweet pickled ginger in sauces for fish and chicken.

2 pounds fresh ginger
½ cup salt
4 cups rice vinegar
3 cups sugar
1 sliced beet

Peel and thinly slice ginger. Toss sliced ginger with salt and leave at room temperature for 1 hour. Rinse salt off ginger. Place remaining ingredients in pan with ginger and simmer gently until ginger is tender and beginning to become translucent. Remove beet slices, pack in a jar and store in fridge. The beet is for naturally colouring the ginger a lovely pink.

Soya-maple glazed smoked mackerel served on a timbale of Yukon Gold potato, avocado, red onion and coriander

Another version using wild Baffin Island Arctic char

CTP/JMP

Fleur de sel caramels

Preparing the store for the Christmas season

CTP/JMP

Gatineau Valley lamb and apple curry with bananas
and poppadum on fragrant Basmati rice

Hazelnut dacquoise with prune and Armaganc sorbet

The delicate task of making caramel twists

December

Huge snowflakes defy gravity with their unhurried, noiseless descent from the sky. Flake by flake the landscape is transformed. Frozen vegetation is gilded and then covered with snow. As the snow continues to fall it first takes on the contours of the land and then of wind as it creates a blanket of soft curves and undulations around Les Fougères.

This is the way we come upon the start of December – usually the arrival time of the first pristine snow that doesn't melt away. After the grey days of November, the brightening brought on by the clean white snow is uplifting. We are filled with a sense of renewal and energy and are reminded of how fortunate we are to enjoy four such very different seasons.

We are thrown into a whirlwind of putting up traditional Christmas decorations, preparing for parties in the restaurant and continuing to try to keep the store fully stocked with delicious and distinctive foods and gifts for festive giving and entertaining.

This season, especially the last two weeks before Christmas, gives everyone an invitation to gather and break bread together. In all our busy lives, times around the table with people who are special to us are precious moments of intimacy. This is the time to talk, laugh, cry, share, argue, resolve, compromise or whatever is necessary to push the truth out in our lives. Almost more than any other place this happens around a table and a meal. As well as being hopelessly food obsessed and feeling that fine food and wine in themselves are uplifting, it is the belief that the table is an important lynchpin in relationships and wellbeing which drew us to devote ourselves to trying to create a distinctive country restaurant. We try to offer people a lovely place and space where Nature's peace and beauty are close at hand, where the welcome and hospitality is warm and genuine, and where the food and wine are special. In other words, we are trying to offer something of an oasis which has the possibility of making a difference by helping to nourish both body and soul. This is what it is all about for us and why Les Fougères is, to us, a meaningful and worthwhile life project.

This month the dining room is full of the camaraderie and song of Christmas gatherings. The store is bustling with people and the air is filled with the mouthwatering juniper and clove aromas of never-ending tourtière-making.

On Christmas Eve the restaurant closes but the store is open for half a day for last-minute shoppers and friends who drop by for a glass of wine and some Brie de Meaux. Then abruptly after this very busy stretch we close until after Boxing Day.

The days running up to New Year's Eve make for another busy week and we also begin to prepare the basic stocks, sauces and garnishes for our special ten-course New Year's Eve menu. On the morning of the 31st there are scarlet cardinals and chickadees in the suet ball-decorated Christmas tree on the verandah. By evening, the restaurant is filled with balloons and live jazz and a long, glorious evening of gastronomy, wines and dancing unfolds. The snow is falling gently through the floodlit woodland. We are connected to all that is universal and timeless with every flake of falling snow. We have our bearings and a new year dawns.

Christmas Cocktail

This is an excellent apéritif as it is based on fruit and wine rather than spirits, so it will not "spoil" or numb the palate before a special meal. It features Neige ice cider, another distinctive and beautiful Québec product from the Hemmingford region.

It was created for us by internationally acclaimed and award winning sommelier (and our former sommelier and manager) Véronique Rivest.

For each serving:
1 ounce Neige ice cider
3½ ounces sparkling wine
   or champagne
½ ounce cranberry juice

Place champagne flutes on ice or in the freezer to chill.

Pour Neige into chilled champagne flute. Top with sparkling wine and cranberry juice. Garnish with 2 frozen cranberries in each glass.

Suet Balls for Birds

In the cold winter months, suet is important in providing fuel in a bird's diet for energy and warmth. We hang our suet balls in the dense shrubbery of outside Christmas trees and other permanent firs because there are lots of places for birds to perch while they feed. The sight of red-ribboned suet balls in our big Christmas tree on the porch with winter birds flitting in and out is magical.

1 cup melted beef suet,
   slightly chilled
1 cup crunchy peanut
   butter

1 cup rolled oats
1 cup cornmeal
1 cup mixed seed for
   wild birds

Mix all ingredients together and form into balls with a looped string for hanging anchored into the middle of each suet ball. As a Christmas decoration, add a red ribbon wired to the top of each ball.

Grilled Venison with Wassail Jus

6 servings

"Wassail" from Medieval Olde England means to toast others with mulled wine or cider and with wishes of good health during winter celebrations such as Christmas, New Year's Eve and Twelfth Night. Mulled wine is essentially hot wine with spices and fruits such as nutmeg, cinnamon, juniper, oranges and currants. Here we are using a spiced wine and brown stock reduction to sauce the venison – the juniper especially partners perfectly with the meat and the dish is very fragrant and festive.

12 thin escalopes of
    venison leg ($2\frac{1}{2}$ ounces
    each)

Marinade

1 cup vegetable oil
$\frac{1}{3}$ cup white wine
$\frac{1}{3}$ cup balsamic vinegar
3 garlic cloves, chopped
2 sprigs thyme
3 bay leaves
1 tbsp crushed juniper
    berries
1 tsp crushed black
    peppercorns

Whisk together marinade ingredients. Marinate escalopes for up to 2 hours. Drain well before grilling. Grill on high heat about 30 seconds per side.

Wassail jus

3 thick slices of orange

4 cloves

2 cups brown stock*

1½ cups red wine

1 tsp crushed juniper
  berries

1 tsp allspice berries

1 tsp grated nutmeg

1 ″ cinnamon stick

2 whole star anise

1 apple, sliced

2 tbsp raisins

⅓ cup balsamic
  vinegar

⅓ cup red currant
  jelly

½ cup red currants or
  raisins

Stud orange slices with cloves (push cloves through peel).

Combine brown stock with red wine, spices, orange slices, apple and raisins in a large pot. Simmer gently over medium-low heat for about ½ hour, until a good flavour is achieved. Strain and discard solids. Return to heat and add balsamic vinegar and red currant jelly. Simmer until jelly is dissolved. Stir in red currants or raisins

To serve:

Nap grilled venison with wassail jus. Dauphinoise potatoes and braised fennel would be a nice accompaniment.

*To make brown stock: Roast 3 pounds of venison or beef bones in a hot oven (450°F) until well browned, adding 1 cup tomato paste and 2 chopped onions, 1 chopped carrot, 1 leek (chopped and rinsed) and 1 chopped celery stalk halfway through. Place browned bones and vegetables into a heavy stockpot. Deglaze the roasting pan with a little water, scraping up all the brown bits, and add to the stockpot. Cover the bones with water and add 1 tsp peppercorns, 1 tsp fresh thyme and 1 bay leaf. Simmer for 3 hours over low heat, skimming often to remove foam and fat. Strain.

Fig, Pine Nut and Rosemary Cake

One 10" round cake

This is a heavenly cake to slice thinly and partner with blue cheese. Of course, any of the triumvirate of royal blues – Stilton, Roquefort or Gorgonzola – would be perfect, but why not try one of the incredible artisan blues from Québec such as Ciel de Charlevoix or Rassembleu?

A drizzle of the amazing Minus 8 vinegar from Niagara would also not go amiss on this plate. This complex vinegar is named after the temperature at which the grapes are picked (to produce the wine that forms its base) in much the same way as our famous Canadian ice wines are made. The sweet, concentrated juice extracted from these frozen grapes is precious and limited indeed. It is fermented and aged with a mother vinegar starter in French oak. This is Canada's own unique, sweet, tart, complex and deep balsamic-like condiment whose every drop expresses our special climate and wine culture.

$\frac{3}{4}$ cup vegetable oil	Beat together oils and sugar until smooth. Add eggs one at a time.
3 tbsp olive oil	
$\frac{3}{4}$ cup sugar	
3 eggs	Sift together dry ingredients. Beat into egg mixture.
$\frac{1}{2}$ tsp salt	
1 tsp baking powder	Stir in figs, nuts and rosemary.
$\frac{1}{2}$ tsp baking soda	
1 cup whole wheat flour	Pour into greased 10ʺ cake pan and bake at 350°F for about 1 hour or until centre springs back when pressed.
1 tsp cinnamon	
$\frac{1}{2}$ cup chopped dried figs, marinated in port overnight	
$\frac{1}{2}$ cup pine nuts, toasted	
2 tsp chopped rosemary	

Christmas lights glow in the quiet before dinner

Véronique and Louis toast the season with a Christmas Cocktail

Grilled venison with wassail jus

Fig, pinenut and rosemary cake with Ciel de Charlevoix
and Niagara's Minus 8 "ice wine" style vinegar

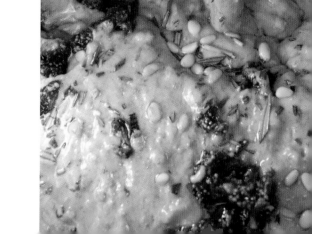

CTP/JWP

And the last plate of the year is served...

New Year's Eve Menu

Torchon of Québec foie gras with duck confit and pistachios
served with a preserved lemon and rosemary jus

∞

Seared Grand Banks scallop on lobster and chorizo risotto
Pinot Gris Hengst 2003 Alsace Grand Cru, Albert Mann

∞

Porcini essence with tarragon and truffle oil
Pinot Noir 2005 Yarra Valley, Coldstream Hills

∞

Apple and Armagnac Trou Normand

∞

Grilled Bison entrecote served with a basil-anchovy butter
and St André Yukon Gold purée, roasted plum tomatoes
with garlic breadcrumbs, aubergine chips and rapini
ou/or
Grilled wild Arctic Char with a pink grapefruit and ginger jus, served on a parsnip
and spinach timbale, buttered leeks and carrot julienne
Zinfandel Old Vine Old Clone 2001 Dry Creek Valley, Alderbrook
Sauvignon Blanc 2006 Marlborough, Babich

∞

Québec artisanal cheeses with homemade
hazelnut crackers and Minus 8 ice wine syrup
La Part des Anges 1997, L'Orpailleur

∞

Dark chocolate almond marjolaine with passionfruit jus
Warre's 10 Year Old Tawny Port

∞

Mignardises

Dégustation Menu

Bay of Fundy Finnan Haddie soup with fragrant spices
and pear, garnished with seared Grand Banks scallop
Malvasia Bianca 2003 Monterey, Ca'del Solo
ဢ

Crispy spiced shrimps served on
coriander creamed corn with a hot red pepper syrup
Gewurztraminer Réserve 2003 Alsace, Dopff & Irion
ဢ

Willy Krauch hot-smoked mackerel, brushed with maple syrup
and served on an avocado and potato timbale
Tokay Pinot Gris 2003 Alsace, Vignerons de Pfaffenheim
ဢ

Okanagan Valley Pinot Blanc and fresh thyme sorbet
ဢ

Seared Québec foie gras with
rhubarb compote and homemade focaccia toast
Riesling Select Late Harvest Indian Summer 2003
Niagara Peninsula, Cave Spring Cellars
ဢ

Veal sweetbreads sautéed with pancetta, red onion and garlic,
deglazed with aged balsamic vinegar and served with roesti potato
Cosme Palacio y Hermanos 2001 Rioja, Bodegas Palacio
ဢ

Grilled Nunavik caribou filet marinated in juniper,
served with a wassail jus and caramelized vegetables
Shiraz 2003 South-Eastern Australia, Rosemount Estate
ဢ

Fig, rosemary & pinenut cake with Ciel de Charlevoix cheese
ဢ

Seasonal fruit tartlet with caramel and fleur de sel ice cream
Moscato d'Asti Nivole 2004, Michele Chiarlo
ဢ

Mignardises

Resources

Groceries & Dry Goods

Asian groceries

Lim Bangkok Groceries
794 Somerset St. W.
Ottawa, ON K1R 6R2
(613) 594-4673

Win Tai Market
1137 Ogilvie Rd.
Ottawa, ON K1J 7P6
(613) 744-2880

Nasa Foods
802 Somerset St. W.
Ottawa, ON K1R 6R5
(613) 234-7226

Kowloon Market
712 Somerset St. W.
Ottawa, ON K1R 6P8
(613) 233-1108

Chocolate, baking ingredients, French gourmet products

Maison Gourmet (wholesale)
20 rue Sicard
Ste-Thérèse, QC J7E 3W7
(450) 628-0202

Nuts

Shiraz Grocery Store
607 Somerset St. W.
Ottawa, ON K1R 5K1
(613) 563-1207

Oils, vinegars, chocolate, fleur de sel, rice, etc.

Itaca Direct & Importations Tribeca (wholesale)
7335 Mile-End
Montréal, QC
H2R 2Z7
www.itacadirect.com
www.tribeca-imports.com
Representative: Margot Silver (613) 748-7975

Organic flour and other organic dry goods

Mountain Path (wholesale)
10755 Pepperville Road
Mountain, ON K0E 1S0
(613) 989-2973
www.mountainpath.com

Pancetta, Parmigiano Reggiano, Italian cheeses, olive oils, vinegars, pasta, etc.

La Bottega Nicastro
64 George Street
Ottawa, ON K1N 5V9
(613) 789-7575
www.labottega.ca

Spices & dry goods

Kurt Schmid Import & Export Inc. (wholesale)
25 rue Audet
Gatineau, QC J8Z 1Y1
(819) 771-9940

St. Ambroise Mustard

Brasserie McAuslan Inc. (wholesale)
5080 rue St-Ambroise
Montreal, QC H4C 2G1
1-800-565-3060
www.mcauslan.com

Meat

General: meat, cheese, produce, etc.

L.A. Distribution (wholesale)
Louis Audet
73 ave. Gatineau
Gatineau, QC J8T 4J4
(819) 568-0462

Boar

Par Toutatis
60 ch. Woods
Farrellton QC
(819) 459-1881

Beef

Priest Creek Farms
Nielon Donovan & Tammy McGarry
438 Chemin du Pont
Poltimore (Val des Monts), QC
J8N 3B1
(819) 457-2563
www.priestcreekfarms.com

Cured meats (bacon, sausage, etc.)

Continental Delicatessen
57 York Street
Ottawa, ON K1N 5B7
(613) 241-7025

Boucanerie Chelsea Smokehouse
706 Route 105
Chelsea, QC J9B 1L2
(819) 827-1925

Duck, geese, foie gras

Aux Champs d'Elise (wholesale)
114 chemin du Vide
Marieville, QC J3M 1N9
www.auxchampsdelise.com
info@auxchampsdelise.com

Élevages Perigord (wholesale)
St-Louis de Gonzague, QC
(450) 377-8766
elevperg@rocler.qc.ca

Mariposa Farms (wholesale & retail)
6468 County Road 17
Plantagenet, ON
K0B 1L0
(613) 673-5881
www.mariposa-duck.on.ca

Game meats

Les Gibiers Canabec (wholesale)
2522 rue de la Faune
C.P. 89036
Saint-Émile, QC G3E 1S9
(418) 843-0782

Grainfed Chicken

La Ferme aux Saveurs des Monts (wholesale)
Sylvain Bertrand
1402 rue Principale
Val-des-Monts, QC J8N 2K5
(819) 457-2828

Lamb

Ferme Bellaar-Spruyt   Ray Cadieux
(819) 459-3138   (613) 673-1804

Venison

Yurtland Farms
Peter and Erica Yurt
308 Route 500 West
Casselman Ontario K0A 1M0
(613) 764-3825

Wild caribou

hunted by First Nations in Nunavik
distributed through Les Gibiers Canabec

Wild hare

trapped in Québec
processed and inspected by La Maison du Lièvre
distributed through Les Gibiers Canabec

Fish

Fish and seafood, partridgeberries

Lapointe Fish Ltd.
445 Catherine Street
Ottawa, ON K1R 5T7
(613) 233-6221
(various retail locations across Ottawa)
www.lapointefish.ca

Smoked mackerel

J. Willy Krauch & Sons Ltd.
P.O. Box 81
Tangier, NS
B0J 3H0
(902) 772-2188
willykrauch@ns.sympatico.ca
(available from Lapointe Fish)

Smoked haddock

Ocean Organic Ltd.
P.O. Box 106,
Yarmouth Co.
Tusket, NS B0W 3M0
(902) 648-3091
(available through Lapointe Fish)

Wild Arctic char, Northern halibut, ice prawns

Pangnirtung Fisheries (wholesale)
P.O. Box 185
Pangnirtung, NU X0A 0R0
(867) 473-8322

Bread

Ace Bakery
1 Hafis Road
Toronto, ON M6M 2V6
(416) 241-3600
1-800-443-7929
www.acebakery.com
bread@acebakery.com
distributed through Tracey's Dairy & Ice Cream Products 1-866-532-3196

Au Pain d'Alain
53 blvd Saint-Joseph
Gatineau, QC J8Y 3W1
(819) 595-6917
www.paindalain.com

Art-Is-In Bakery
Kevin Mathieson
(819) 639-1434
www.art-is-in-bakery.com

Produce

Farm Produce

Bristol Heritage Farms
Tjeerd Vandanberg
45 Fifth Line
Bristol, QC J0X 1G0
(819) 647-3820
1-866-205-0001

Juniper Farm
Alex Mackay-Smith and Juniper Turgeon
460 Kalalla Road
Alcove, QC J0X 1A0
(819) 422-1894
fermejuniper@yahoo.ca

Honey

Berg en Dal Honey Farm
R.R. #1
Alcove, QC J0X 1A0
(819) 459-3539
www.bergendalhoney.com
bergendalhoneyfarm@yahoo.com

Jeff Schultz Apiaries
C-57 Bryson Rd. R.R. #1
Shawville, QC J0X 2Y0
(819) 647-3665

Maple syrup & maple sugar

Erablière Claude Laplante
53 Val-du-Lac Road
St-Pierre-de-Wakefield, QC J8N 2R1
(819) 457-9223
www.organic-storyteller.ca/erabliere.htm

Mushrooms

Les Champignons Le Coprin (wholesale)
Christophe Marineau
C.P. 402
Wakefield, QC J0X 3G0
(819) 664-8030
christophe@lecoprin.ca

Coffee & Tea

Coffee and supplies

Morala Trading
1320 Bank Street
Ottawa, ON K1S 3Y4
(613) 737-9838
1-800-625-9625
www.morala.com

Coffee - Fair Trade

Café La Brûlerie/Maison de Torréfaction
152 Montcalm
Gatineau, QC J8X 2M2
(819) 778-0109
cafelabrulerie@videotron.ca

Bean Fair
P.O. Box 97
Wakefield, QC
(819) 459-4452
beanfair@magma.ca

Teas

Harney & Sons
5723 Route 22
Millerton, NY 12546
1-800-TEA-TIME
www.harney.com

Québec Cheeses

Québec artisanal cheeses

descriptions and links can be found at www.fromagesduquebec.qc.ca

Au Gré des Champs, Montérégie
(450) 346-8732   www.augredeschamps.com

Ferme Floralpe, Papineauville
(819) 427-5700   floralpe@hotmail.com

Fromage Côté, Warwick
www.fromagescote.com

Fromagerie de l'Ile-aux-Grues, Chaudières-Appalaches
(418) 248-5842

La Fromagerie Lehmann, Hébertville, Lac St-Jean
(418) 344-1414

La Fromagerie Médard, St-Gédéon, Lac St-Jean
(418) 345-2407   fromagerie_medard@hotmail.com

Fromagerie du Pied-De-Vent, Iles-de-la-Madeleine
(418) 969-9292   piedvent@tlb.sympatico.ca

Les Fromagiers de la Table Ronde, Ste-Sophie, Laurentides
(450) 530-2436   www.fromagiersdelatableronde.qc.ca

La Maison Alexis de Portneuf
1-866-901-3312   www.alexisdeportneuf.com

Le Mouton Blanc, La Pocatière, Bas St-Laurent
(418) 856-6627   le.mouton.blanc@sympatico.ca

La Suisse Normande, Lanaudière
(450) 588-6503   la-suisse-normande@sympatico.ca

Eggs

Bekings Poultry Farm
R.R. #1
Oxford Station, ON K0G 1T0
(613) 258-5396

Seeds

Canadian Seed Growers Association
seeds@seedgrowers.ca
www.seedgrowers.ca

The Cook's Garden
1-800-457-9703
www.cooksgarden.com
(Pennsylvania, USA)

Johnny's Selected Seeds
1-877-564-6697
www.johnnyseeds.com
(Maine, USA)

Miscellaneous

Glycerin for preserving

Over-the-counter item available in most well-stocked pharmacies

Neige Ice Cider

Cidrerie La Face Cachée de la Pomme
617 Route 202
Hemmingford, QC J0L 1H0
(450) 247-2899
www.cidredeglace.com

Minus 8 Vinegar

Minus 8 Inc.
6 Park Avenue
St. Catharines, ON L2P 1R1
minus8vinegar@yahoo.ca

Woodworking & Cabinetry

Richard Blais
(819) 455-9459
(613) 828-9145

1994

photo VanBeek

photo VanBeek

2007

1993

1986   2007